W9-BYY-937

BARRON'S PARENTING KEYS

KEYS TO PARENTING YOUR THREE YEAR OLD

Susan E. Gottlieb, M.D.

Sellersburg Library
430 N. Indiana Avenue
Sellersburg, IN 47172

DISCARDED

Charlestown--Clark Co. Public Library
51 Clark Road
Charlestown, IN 47111

BARRON'S

Cover photo by Scott Barrow, Inc., Cold Spring, NY

DEDICATION

To the students, families, and staff of the Decatur-Clearpool School—working toward the dream
And to Ali—La mouse!

Copyright ©1995 by Barron's Educational Series, Inc.

All rights reserved.
No part of this book may be reproduced in any form, by photostat, microfilm, xerography, or any other means, or incorporated into any information retrieval system, electronic or mechanical, without the written permission of the copyright owner.

All inquiries should be addressed to:
Barron's Educational Series, Inc.
250 Wireless Boulevard
Hauppauge, New York 11788

Library of Congress Catalog Card No.: 94-38321

International Standard Book No. 0-8120-1417-0

Library of Congress Cataloging-in-Publication Data
Gottlieb, Susan E.
　Keys to parenting your three year old / Susan E. Gottlieb.
　　p. cm.—(Barron's parenting keys)
　Includes index.
　1. Toddlers. 2. Child rearing. 3. Parenting. I. Title. II. Series.

HQ774.5.G675　1995　　　　　　　　　　　94-38321
649'.123—dc20　　　　　　　　　　　　　　CIP

PRINTED IN THE UNITED STATES OF AMERICA

5678　8800　987654321

CONTENTS

INTRODUCTION

A s a pediatrician, I've always wanted to specialize in three year olds. Writing this book has been the next best thing. Three year olds are at a wonderful point in their development. They have mastered the basics of mobility, communication, and self-care. They feel good about themselves and their accomplishments. They are eager to please, curious, even tempered, and optimistic.

This book has been designed to provide a comprehensive view of the three year old. It looks at his or her life as an individual, a member of a family, and a part of a community.

Part One is devoted to the child's inner life. It covers motor, language, and emotional development, cognitive abilities, and temperamental style.

Part Two considers the child in the context of the family. Practical issues, such as feeding, sleep, play, and safety, are addressed. This section also explores such topics as discipline, relationships, self-esteem, becoming a sibling, and behavior problems. Many parents want to know what they can do to enhance their child's development. Several chapters in this section focus on ways to raise a child who is bright, creative, and interested in learning.

Three year olds also function in a wider world. They may move to a new home, travel, host a birthday party, enter preschool, or encounter people who are different. These situations are discussed in Part Three.

The descriptions in this book portray the average three year old. They are not intended to be rigid timetables. Variations in development are expected. Some children develop in spurts; others develop more gradually. All children have their own patterns of strengths and weaknesses and may progress more easily in one area than in another. Concerns about an individual child's development or behavior should be brought to the attention of the pediatrician.

Life with a three year old is a glorious adventure. He or she brings a refreshingly unique point of view to relationships, natural phenomena, and everyday situations. Seeing the world through the eyes of a three year old is amusing, surprising, and enriching. I hope that this book will add to the joy of knowing a three-year-old child.

1

GROSS MOTOR DEVELOPMENT

In the playground, Naomi is in constant motion. She pedals her tricycle furiously, deftly steering it around parked strollers and unsteady toddlers. Then she dismounts, climbs the ladder to the slide, and descends with a gleeful shriek. Her next challenge is to walk around the raised border of the sandbox. She is only able to do this for a few paces until she loses her balance and jumps into the sand. "Ding, ding," the bell from the ice-cream truck sounds. Naomi picks herself up and gallops off to get money for a treat.

Three year olds derive much pleasure from activities involving the large muscle groups of the arms and legs. Exercise has obvious benefits in improving strength, coordination, and flexibility. It also help children's confidence and pride as they see their bodies perform in new ways. They remember when they were not able to ride a tricycle or balance on one foot. New skills are mastered in quick succession during this very important time in physical development.

Locomotion Commotion

Posture clearly distinguishes the three year old from the toddler. A three year old stands straighter. Her abdomen is less prominent, giving her a leaner appearance.

A three year old's walk is graceful. It is much like an adult's, with erect shoulders and a rhythmic arm swing. She can walk forward, backward, and sideways. She can even stand on tiptoe.

Running is even more fun than walking. Three year olds run smoothly, in contrast to the stiff-legged gait of the two year old. Three year olds are able to start and stop precisely and turn corners. Three year olds also like to gallop. Galloping is a loping movement with the same foot always leading and the other foot closing in from behind.

Three year olds have the ability to jump with both feet. They can generally get about 12 inches off the ground. They love to jump from the bottom step of the staircase. Once this is mastered, they will try to clear two, three, or four steps.

Stair climbing is a skill that improves during this period. Three year olds are able to alternate feet when walking up a flight of stairs. They may still be placing two feet on each tread while descending. Climbing skills are also evident on playground apparatus, such as slides and jungle gyms.

Riding a tricycle is one of the three year old's proudest achievements. A tricycle is much more like a real bicycle than any of the scooter toys favored by two year olds. A three year old can pedal and can competently steer around most obstacles. Tricycles are also important in imaginative play, in which they may serve as fire engines or ice-cream trucks.

Balancing Act

Balance undergoes rapid improvement in this age group. A three year old is able to stand on one leg for a brief time. She may be able to hop a few times. By four, she is able to hop with ease. Half of three year olds can walk forward for a distance of

10 feet without straying from a 1-inch line. A three year old can walk for a short distance on a balance beam.

Take Me Out to the Ball Game

Ball play remains a popular pastime. A three year old's new skills add to the fun. She can throw overhand for a distance of 10 feet. She can can kick a ball with substantial force. A three year old catches a ball with stiffly outstretched arms. She has more success with a ball that is bounced to her than one thrown on a fly.

Activities

Three year olds naturally find ways to use their large muscles. The following suggestions provide some special kinds of fun.

Children love to dance. They enjoy all kinds of pop, folk, and classical music. Introduce them to different instruments and a variety of tempos. Allow the children to develop their imaginations by moving like robots, snakes, bears, mice, or their favorite animals. Demonstrate a funny new movement, and have the children imitate it. This kind of activity teaches about observation and following directions as well as movement.

Children love to toss beanbags at a target. Beanbags can be handmade, and a cardboard box suffices as a target. This is a good rainy day alternative to baseball in the living room.

Large motor activity is a wonderful outlet for a three year old's boundless energy.

2

~~~~~~

FINE MOTOR DEVELOPMENT

It was too quiet in Edgar's room. Mrs. Cintron strolled over to his doorway to have a peek. What was keeping her usually energetic son so busy?

She smiled as she saw him huddled over, deeply absorbed in his task. She called his name in a gentle voice to avoid startling him. But she was the one to be startled! As Edgar averted his head, she saw patches of jagged stubble where his beautiful red curls used to be and a large pair of silvery scissors in his hand.

The three year old's command of small finger movements opens up an exciting new world. He finds pleasure in painting, puzzles, and play doughs. Not only are these activities fun, but they enable him to practice the movements he will need later for writing.

Picasso, Matisse, and Klee

A three year old can draw a circle. Instead of the multiple circular scribbles he did at two, he can now stop after a single revolution. By $3\frac{1}{2}$, he will be able to draw intersecting lines and copy a cross. By four, he will draw a square or rectangle with recognizable corners. In addition to being able to draw the figures more precisely, he is also now able to place them where he wants them on the page.

At this age, children are more adept at designs than they are at the human figure. Drawings of people are still quite basic. They may consist only of a face with two additional features.

Even the crayon stroke itself has undergone a transformation. In contrast to the toddler's tentative markings, the three year old's firm grip produces a bold line. It is still normal for a child of this age to hold the crayon in a clenched fist rather than between the thumb and index finger. The child experiments with different positions as he searches for one that provides both comfort and control. The shift to a mature grip usually takes place between ages three and four.

Most three year olds demonstrate a clear preference for either the right or the left hand. Some children take a little longer than others to decide. Many of the children who take their time turn out to be left-handed.

Puzzles, Blocks, and Beads

Three year olds can perform skills that require greater hand-eye coordination. They complete puzzles by visually matching the pieces with the available spaces. This strategy differs from the trial-and-error approach they used as two year olds. They turn the puzzle pieces around now rather than relentlessly hammering something that does not fit. They can tackle a simple inlay puzzle in which three to five pieces interlock to make the final design. By four they may be able to complete a puzzle with as many as 30 pieces.

They can stack nine or ten 1-inch cubes to make a tower. Their placement of the blocks is accurate and deft. They can also copy a model of a three-cube bridge.

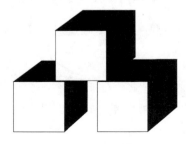

Three year olds can learn to string beads or other objects. Stringing involves the coordination of both hands in a series of pushing, pulling, and holding maneuvers. This process can be made a bit less frustrating if the free end of the lace is stiffened with glue or a piece of tape. Once mastered, stringing is a source of great delight. Parents will be the proud recipients of many elegant necklaces of painted dry pasta or breakfast cereal.

Using Tools

The three year old looks forward to using common household tools, such as scissors, hammers, and knives. Tools must be used under supervision. A three year old's judgment is not as advanced as his dexterity. Edgar might have had a much more radical haircut had his mother not been as vigilant.

Cutting is a skill that requires practice. Give the child newspapers, magazines, or catalogs to cut. An easy project for a beginner is to cut a fringe around the edges of a piece of construction paper. By the end of the fourth year, the child should be able to cut a straight line. Cutting a curved line and cutting around the outline of an object come later. Choose a pair of special training scissors for the child. Training scissors are safer and easier for small hands to manipulate.

Rotary movement can be practiced using an eggbeater. Eggbeaters can whip cream, soap suds, or plain water.

Activities

Three year olds readily engage in fine motor activities. These activities allow children to be creative and expressive. They also help children develop the dexterity they need for writing. Source books for all of the activities mentioned can be found under Activity Books for Adults.

Messy Activities

Working with play doughs involves the fine motor actions of squeezing, poking, and rolling. Doughs can be purchased or prepared at home inexpensively. They can be enhanced with food colorings or aromatic oils. Even edible doughs can be made using peanut butter as a base.

Similar skills can be developed through cooking activities. Give the child his own piece of dough to work with, or let him assist the main chef. There is a wonderful sense of accomplishment when those fragrant muffins come out of the oven.

Painting can be done with a traditional brush or a cotton swab, a tree branch, or a finger. Printing with fruit is a satisfying activity now that children can really control where the design goes on the page.

Collage is a popular activity, probably because it involves playing with glue. Children love making designs as they squirt the glue onto the paper. Tinted glue makes it even more fun. This is a great way to get rid of odd pieces of fabric, yarn, tissue paper, and gift wrap. Children enjoy deciding which materials to use and where to place them on the page. Theme collages, featuring only purple objects or items beginning with the letter *a*, add an educational component.

Water play is creative and calming. An added advantage is that children can learn about pouring, measuring, and mixing.

Nonmessy Activities

Three year olds love finger plays, the hand movements that accompany songs or chants. Finger plays enhance fine motor coordination and also help children remember the words.

Another way to develop hand coordination skills is to introduce signs from the American Sign Language used by the hearing impaired. Children love the idea of learning a special new language. This also gives them an appreciation of the complexity of being different.

Three year olds can cut paper, or they can cut hair. The challenge is to provide them with suitable outlets for developing and elaborating their skills.

3

~~~~~~

LANGUAGE DEVELOPMENT

Mr. Furman, the preschool teacher, reprimanded Hailey for running in the classroom. "Calm down or you'll have to sit in the time-out chair," he said. Hailey glared at her teacher. "I'm going to turn you into an eensy, beensy, teeny, weeny, little spider," she responded.

A greater sophistication in language usage is one of the hallmarks of the three year old. Language continues to develop in very dramatic ways during the fourth year.

Using Language

A three year old uses language for a variety of purposes.

She uses words to comment on and describe her world. ("I have a pink pony.") She can specify relationships between objects. ("My pony is bigger than yours.") She can talk about location using such prepositions as on, next to, or under. ("My doll is riding on top of the pony.")

She can express negation. ("I can't sleep.") This is much more specific than the toddler's phrase "no sleep," which could mean "I don't want to sleep anymore," "I won't sleep," or "I can't sleep."

She can use language to control behavior and express emotions. She can say "stop it" instead of hitting a child who is annoying her. The phrase "I'm angry" replaces the tantrum when she can't get her way. "I'm sad" brings the desired hug more quickly than a torrent of tears.

Three year olds learn to signify quantities greater than 1 by adding an *s* to the nouns that they already know. Their universal application of this rule leads to the charming ungrammatical forms characteristic of this age, such as "mans" instead of "men" and "mouses" instead of "mice."

A three year old uses language to obtain information. How do you make light bulbs? Do octopuses have scales? Why do bubbles pop? A child of this age can ask up to 400 questions a day. Sometimes the child really knows the answer. Then the fun is in controlling and prolonging the conversation by greeting each statement with, "But why?"

Three year olds can put several sentences together to tell a familiar story in a logical sequence. They should be able to convey a simple message.

Language is also critical to pretend play. A child needs language to develop the narrative that gives play its form. This is true whether the play is solitary play with animal or human figures, puppet dialogs, or dramatic play with peers. A child may even disguise her voice or adopt an accent in an act of inspired linguistic playfulness.

What's in a Word?

A three year old loves words. Her vocabulary ranges between 250 and 1,000 words. A 1,000-word vocabulary encompasses the names of almost all the objects in the child's environment. She also knows some action and descriptive words. By $3\frac{1}{2}$ the child's vocabulary expands to between 1,200 words and 1,800 words, and it reaches 1,800 to 2,500 by age four. In counting a child's vocabulary, only words used in spontaneous conversation are included. The number of words she actually understands is far greater. She adores using sophisticated words, such as *secret, surprise,* and *spectacular.* She enjoys rhyming words. She can sing the lyrics to simple songs and recite nursery rhymes.

By $3\frac{1}{2}$, a child becomes aware that there are words in the English language that sound the same but have different meanings. "Watch" can indicate a timepiece or a verb synonymous with "see."

She also starts to understand words related to time. The announcement of a relative's upcoming visit might prompt, "I didn't see Uncle Bud for a long time." A child can be stalled with such phrases as "it's not time now" or "we'll do it later." Parents must then be prepared for the question, "Is it later yet?"

At three, the average sentence is three to five words in length. By $3\frac{1}{2}$, sentences are already appreciably longer. She can use the personal pronoun *I.* A $3\frac{1}{2}$ year old uses auxiliary verbs, such as *could, would,* and *can.* She can use the past tense but has difficulty with irregular verbs. ("I buyed my pony at the toy store.")

Receptive Language

It is also important to consider what a child understands when other people talk to her. This is a child's *receptive language ability.*

A three year old should be able to follow a three-step direction. ("Please place the tape in the VCR, turn on the television, and come sit next to me.")

Three year olds should also be able to answer simple questions. They should be able to state their first and last names and say whether they are a boy or a girl. They should be able to describe what they would do if they were tired, hungry, or cold.

Wabbits and Woosters

A three year old's pronunciation is rarely perfect. Her speech is considered adequate if 75% of it can be understood by a listener who is not part of the family. Virtually everything she says should be intelligible to her parents.

During the fourth year, the child works on the p, b, m, w, h, k, th, and f sounds. Substitutions, such as "baf" for "bath," "dis" for "this," and "thun" for "sun," are common and require no intervention.

How Parents Can Help

Parents are extremely influential in the area of language development. Children model their language on the language they hear around them. Speaking with children and reading to them provide the good language models that are needed for optimal development.

Most three year olds love to talk. Parents can aid in the development of self-expression by becoming patient, active, and available conversational partners. This means exchanging ideas rather than merely giving orders. Ask the child her opinion, and then really stop and listen to her answer. Having an adult's undivided attention adds to a child's self-esteem. "If an adult is really listening to me," the child thinks, "then I must be important!"

Questions help children develop their critical thinking skills. Try to phrase questions in a way that requires more than a yes or no answer. "What was your favorite part of the story?" elicits more information than "Did you like the story?" When children are telling stories, such questions as "Then what happened?" and "Can you tell me more?" help them focus on sequence and detail. "How did you feel then?" reminds children to recognize and express emotions verbally rather than physically.

Stuttering

Dysfluency, or stuttering, is a common language problem seen in the middle of the fourth year. Stuttering involves the repetition of whole words, parts of words, or even entire phrases. It is thought that stuttering emerges at this time because the child is formulating words faster than she can actually express them. This type of stuttering is not caused by emotional problems, although stress can make it worse.

Normal dysfluency lasts two to three months. It is not necessarily present every day. What parents can do during this period is provide an accepting environment for expression. They must remain calm and avoid the temptation to jump in and supply the word when the child becomes stuck; otherwise, her confidence is eroded. Asking her to slow down, practice certain words, or start a phrase over will not curtail the stuttering. Because dysfluency is involuntary, punishing the child or showing disapproval will not help. Another important part of establishing a supportive environment is making sure the child is not teased by her siblings.

Certain behaviors indicate a more serious type of stuttering. If a child becomes very self-conscious, avoids talking, grimaces, or has repetitive facial movements (*tics*) along with the stuttering, a thorough medical and language evaluation is in order. Stuttering that lasts longer than six months should also be investigated.

Delayed Language Development

Although the range of language abilities is wide, all children must meet certain criteria.

A three year old should be speaking in at least three-word sentences. She should be able to understand a simple story. More than 75% of her speech should be understandable to an unfamiliar adult.

By four a child should speak in sentences longer than five words, refer to herself as *I*, listen to longer stories, tell a simple story, identify actions depicted in pictures, know her first and last names, age, and street, and be fully intelligible to people outside the immediate family.

A child who does not meet these criteria should be seen by her pediatrician and referred to a speech pathologist or other specialist for a thorough evaluation, including a hearing test. Much of language development takes place in the first few years of life. Getting help early allows her to make the most of these critical early years.

There are impediments to obtaining appropriate care. Parents sometimes ignore a language problem, hoping it will disappear on its own. They may be falsely reassured by anecdotes about other children who just "grew out of it." They may delay seeking help out of guilt, shame, or fear that their child will be labeled retarded.

It is hard to face the possibility of a developmental problem, but parents must remember that the child depends on them to act in her best interest. Talk to the pediatrician, and work together to develop a plan for evaluation and treatment.

Watching a three year old grow in language competence is one of the unparalleled joys of the fourth year.

4

THINKING

Lily was looking for something to use to string beads. Her mother gave her a ball of purple yarn. "Thanks for the string," Lily said. "That actually isn't string," her mother explained, "It's called yarn. It comes from the wool that sheep make." Lily looked puzzled. "But I've never seen a purple sheep," she said.

A world that can produce yarn in any color of the rainbow is taken for granted by adults, but it is something marvelous to a three year old. A three year old encounters unfamiliar objects and ideas every day. She is constantly readjusting her understanding of the world as she incorporates new information. Every interaction is an opportunity for discovery. Even an innocent request for string can lead to a thrilling revelation.

A three year old does not see the world in the same way that an adult does. She does not share all adult assumptions. She does not yet ascribe to the laws governing cause and effect, time, and physical matter. She does not accept the prevailing rules of logic. Her special way of thinking can lead to frustrating or hilarious consequences. It is certainly never dull. As parents share the joy of discovery with their three year old, they find themselves looking at the world with a renewed sense of wonder.

Concrete Thinking

"Concrete" is a term used to describe a three year old's thinking. Concrete in this context means that they understand what they touch, what they see, and what they experience.

This accounts for Lily's bafflement with the wool. She knew that wool came from sheep. She had seen black sheep and white sheep on a visit to a farm. In her scheme, therefore, black wool and white wool made sense. But how could she account for purple wool? It did not fit her understanding of direct translation from sheep to wool. She was unable to conceive of dyeing the wool because it was just too big a leap from her experience.

Magical Thinking

Three year olds engage in magical thinking. They believe that their thoughts and wishes can influence events. Seth sometimes wished that his annoying younger brother, Jonah, didn't exist. One day Jonah really did disappear when he became separated from the rest of the family at the mall. Seth saw this as evidence of the power of his thoughts, although an adult would rightly classify this as a coincidence.

Three year olds do not understand cause and effect. They believe that events linked in time have a causal relationship. Seth broke a household rule when he threw a toy at his brother. Jonah sustained a large bruise above his eye. Later that day Seth came down with an earache and a fever. Seth believed that his illness was a punishment for having hit his brother. For three-year-old Seth, two events that happened that close together had to be related.

Egocentricity

A three year old feels that she is the center of the universe. This egocentricity leads her to think that events occur in nature for her benefit. The waves lap up on the shore to play with her, and the sun rises each morning to keep her warm.

Egocentricity should not be confused with selfishness. It is not that a three year old refuses to consider the viewpoints of others. Rather, she has not yet developed the flexibility of thinking that allows her to do so.

This is why it is ineffective to ask a three-year-old child who bites or hits others, "How would you like it if someone did that to you?" She can't possibly conceptualize how it would feel to be the other person. She can't modify her behavior out of consideration for someone else. At this age, she is concerned only for herself.

Animism

A three year old does not distinguish between animate and inanimate objects. She doesn't understand why petals can't be glued back on a flower the way a handle can be reattached to a broken cup. She attributes human feelings to things that are not alive. If she trips on the curb, it is the bad sidewalk that was responsible for her fall.

Temporal Thinking

Time is a difficult subject for a young child to grasp. A three year old understands time as it pertains to her daily schedule. She knows the sequence of activities that comprises her day. She associates morning with school and evening with her parents' return from work.

During the fourth year she begins to understand the concepts of today, tomorrow, and yesterday. A calendar can help make these relationships clear. Longer time intervals are incomprehensible to the three year old. A child who goes to school Monday through Friday becomes confused when the weekend comes. Just when she's adjusted to the weekend timetable, Monday arrives again. A lengthy vacation is an even greater puzzle.

Conservation

Three year olds believe what they see. This is the conclusion of a series of ingenious experiments designed by the Swiss psychologist Jean Piaget. He was interested in knowing what young children understand about objects undergoing changes in their appearance.

One task starts with equal amounts of water in two identical cups. As the child watches, the contents of one cup is poured into a tall skinny vase. The water in the other cup is poured into a short squat vase, also in the child's view. The absolute amount of water is unchanged, yet a three year old will say that there is more water in the tall vase because its water level is higher.

Another task features two equal lumps of clay. The child watches as one is left in a ball and the other is rolled into a long skinny snake. A three year old insists that the snake has more clay. She cannot discount the impression made by its length.

These experiments show that three year olds cannot conserve matter. They do not realize that superficial changes in form do not signify changes in amount. Even when the transformations are made before their eyes, three year olds trust their perception over logic.

What They Know

By the end of the fourth year, the child should have a basic understanding of color, shape, and size.

Color is an abstract concept. It is first learned through matching. A fun game is to glue paper of different colors to the bottom of each section of a muffin tin. Cut up some additional scraps of paper, and have the child sort them according to color. The child can make a color collage with pictures cut from magazines. Have a purple day, featuring purple clothes, purple food, and a reading of *Harold and the Purple Crayon*. By four, a child can name the basic colors and at least point to some of the less common colors.

Shape learning is much the same as color learning. Start with some basic shapes (circles, squares, and triangles) cut from construction paper. Have the child sort them. Once she can appreciate the differences, help her learn the names. By four, she should be able to name the basic shapes and match more difficult shapes, such as diamonds or octagons.

A child can count to 4 by rote. She may not actually understand quantities greater than 1 or 2. She can hand over "just 1" or "lots" of objects when asked.

A three year old knows a lot about her world. She can name and point out body parts, including thumb, neck, and stomach. She can explain what a stove is used for and what she would do if she were tired or hungry. She can identify opposites, such as same and different, short and tall, or fast and slow. She can follow a three-part direction. She can recall incidents in a story. By four she can recognize a few important capital letters, such as the first letter in her name.

Encouraging the Thinker

Three year olds are well equipped to add to their store of information. They ask hundreds of questions a day. Simple and direct responses are usually the best. Children are bored by long, drawn-out answers. Be assured that they will ask a follow-up question if they are not satisfied.

Parents don't have to know all the answers. A response such as "I don't know. Let's look it up when we go to the library," is perfectly acceptable.

Parents don't need to do all the work. The question "How do light bulbs work?" can be met with "I don't know. What do you think?" The child needs the experience of pondering a question and taking a chance with an answer. Give her some time to think about it. If she's stuck, give her a hint. Remember to praise her even if she doesn't come up with the right answer. The goal is to launch her as an active learner. As she asks more questions, she adds to her knowledge. As she solves more problems, she gains confidence in her abilities. This helps her approach future challenges in a positive manner.

Seeing the world through the eyes of a three year old brings a fresh appreciation of its beauty and complexity.

5

EMOTIONAL DEVELOPMENT

T he fourth year is a delightful time. After the turbulent twos, lovable and responsive three year olds are a welcome contrast.

The year starts out with a calm, conforming, eager-to-please child who enjoys showing off his new skills. This phase lasts for about six months. At $3\frac{1}{2}$, a shift takes place. The child goes through a period of testing and rebellion. He is withdrawn and strong willed. He can be unpredictable, bossy, whiny, and insecure. He insists on immediate attention. New habits, such as nail biting, boasting, or stuttering, may emerge. Patience and firmness help the child progress through this period. He regains his equilibrium by the time he turns four.

Greater Emotional Maturity

Two factors contribute importantly to the three year old's emotional maturity. One is his increased command of language. He uses words rather than physical actions to express his feelings. He also has the ability to communicate more precisely. The uncompromising "no eat that" of the two year old becomes "that looks yucky." When parents get a glimpse of the child's motivation, they are more likely to respond by negotiating rather than insisting on absolute compliance. Negotiation has a major advantage. It results in two at least partially satisfied parties rather than one smug winner and a loser with bruised feelings.

The other critical influence is identification with the parents. Three year olds want very much to be like their parents. They imitate their parents' speech and actions. They conform to their parents' directions. They do so to win parental praise and affection. Even their tendency toward boasting is explained by their desire to impress their parents.

Greater Emotional Range

Three year olds have an expanded emotional repertoire. The first emotions children experience are happiness, sadness, anger, and fear. In the fourth year, children explore more complex issues, such as dependency, closeness, separation, protest, assertiveness, and self-pride. They are also capable of empathy. This is a time when children go over and try to comfort another child who is crying.

Initiative and Guilt

Erick Erickson characterized this period as a struggle between initiative and guilt. Initiative is seen in a child's exhuberant climb to the top of the jungle gym, the colorful swirls he applies to paper, or his incessant conversation. His actions are purposeful and productive. This contrasts dramatically with the behavior of the two year old, who seeks independence for its own sake. The key to success in this period is to be able to join wholeheartedly in these activities without feeling guilty or impinging on the rights of others.

Sex Role Identification

During this period, children begin to learn about the rules, roles, and responsibilities associated with being a boy or a girl. Children start out wishing for a special relationship with the parent of the opposite sex. This is the time that boys declare that they want to marry their mothers. Girls act coy around their fathers. There is a feeling of competitiveness with the parent of the same sex and resentment of the parents' relationship with each other. Children eventually see the futility of their wish. By the time this phase resolves, children have formed a strong bond with the same-sex parent.

This process is also reflected in pretend play. Boys insist on playing the father, and girls want only to be the mother. Occupations are also assigned in a rigid and stereotyped way, with girls and boys being excluded from certain professions.

Exploring Feelings Through Play

A child explores emotional themes through fantasy play. Parents can learn a lot about what is on a child's mind by observing his play. The key is to watch without taking over or being intrusive. Parents can join in the play if invited to do so by the child.

Gilbert's mother was about to return to her office job after a three year maternity leave. She noticed that her son's play at the time was rife with episodes of separation and reunion. When invited to partake, Gil's mother chose the part of the baby doll. Her doll had a tantrum as he neared the day care center. She was relieved to hear Gil say, "Don't cry. You will have fun in day care. I will pick you up at five."

Feelings can also be explored through group play. Children try on adult roles as they play house, store, or doctor. They learn what it is like to be in charge. Cooperative play also becomes a forum for beginning conflict resolution. The play is so important that children find a way to work out their differences so that it can continue.

Friendships

Stable and enduring friendships are still a thing of the future. Some children prefer to play consistently with one or two other youngsters. Others define a friend as the person they are playing with at the moment. They may drift in and out of many such friendships during the course of a single day.

Children also have imaginary friends. Imaginary friends allow children to try on different feelings. An imaginary friend may be older or of the opposite sex. The friend may even be an animal. Children are then able to experience the world through the eyes of someone who is bold, good at baseball, or fond of green peas.

Children at three experience a wider range of feelings than ever before. Their growing abilities to reason and empathize help them appreciate, enjoy, and control feelings in themselves and in others.

6

~~~~~~

FEARS

Nora was afraid of dogs. If a dog approached her, she would cower behind the nearest adult until it was out of sight.

Charles was fearful of performers in costume. He refused to attend any social gatherings at which he might encounter a clown or a magician.

Avery was afraid of the dark. He had been a model sleeper until the age of $3\frac{1}{2}$. Since this fear developed, his behavior patterns had changed radically. He began fussing at bedtime and waking up several times during the night.

Nora, Charles, and Avery are experiencing fears common to three year olds.

What Are Fears?

Fears are expressions of powerful emotional reactions. It is normal for three year olds to experience fears. Fears are commonly seen in young children because they have not yet developed more sophisticated ways of coping with strong feelings.

Fears can be precipitated by change. They are particularly prominent at age $3\frac{1}{2}$, when many dramatic developments are taking place. Language competence explodes. Imagination soars. Aggressive feelings surface. There are increased expectations for self-care and social behavior. The sum of these new capacities leaves a child feeling anxious, unsettled, and fearful.

Changes in the child's external environment can have a similar impact. A move to a new home, the birth of a sibling, the absence or death of a close relative, a new caregiver, or the start of school can all give rise to fears.

Fears can also have their roots in real-life experiences. A violent or hostile confrontation with a person or an animal can be the source of a child's fears.

There are a few specific entities that three year olds commonly fear. They include animals, loud noises, and the dark. Children fear things they cannot control. They cannot anticipate the way a dog is going to react. They don't understand what caused a loud noise to occur. They don't know what is lurking in a darkened room. Children at this age know how hard it is to control their own aggressive feelings, and they worry about violent forces going unchecked.

Identifying Fears

Expressions of fearfulness can be obvious or subtle. Nora was able to state clearly that she was afraid of dogs. Charles, too, was able to articulate his fear. Avery's parents could tell that he was afraid by the anxious expression on his face.

Fear may be more difficult to detect in other children. Such behaviors as thumb sucking, nail biting, or hair twisting can be signs of fear. There may be changes in children's play, eating, or sleeping patterns. They may act silly or babyish. Another response to fears is to cover up by talking a lot or acting exceptionally brave.

There are some additional actions parents can take if the source of the child's fears is not obvious. Look for a pattern to the child's fears. Do they surface around particular activities or particular people? Is he comfortable at home but different in day care? Encourage the child to talk about his feelings.

27

Reading a book together may help him open up. He may be less reluctant to talk once he realizes that everyone has these kinds of feelings from time to time. A list of suitable books can be found in Resources.

How Parents Can Help

The most important thing a parent can do is to take the child's fears seriously. This is a time when the child needs an extra measure of love, support, and patience. He needs a hug and reassurance that he will be protected.

When a child is scared, no amount of rational talk about how there is nothing to fear in the dark will eradicate his fears. A parent knows that Neville is a sweet dog with a loud bark or that the clown is only trying to get a laugh. The child, however, views the behavior as uncomfortably aggressive. Belittling the child's fears, dismissing them, or telling him to stop acting like a baby only adds to his distress. Now not only does he feel afraid, but he feels misunderstood.

An Action Plan: Clarification

Sometimes fears are based on a misconception. In these cases, clarification may help. This tactic works particularly well, for instance, with the fear of thunder.

Children's fear of thunder is a product of their own immature thinking processes. They have a tendency to attribute human characteristics to inanimate objects. They equate the sound of thunder with an expression of anger. They become scared that they will be the target of the angry feelings.

Some parents counter with a simple scientific explanation; others say that the angels are going bowling. Cuddling up with the child during a storm can turn it into a fun experience. Discuss the benefits of rainfall, or teach the child to count the interval between the lightning and the thunder to track the progress of the storm.

An Action Plan: Desensitization

Nora was miserable about her fear of dogs. Her parents set up a plan to help her. They started by reading picture books about dogs and puppies. Then they visited the local pet shop. At first they just stayed outside and looked at the dogs through the window. After a few weeks, they went to an animal shelter, where the staff selected a gentle animal for Nora to handle. Eventually she was able to accompany a neighbor when he walked his dog down their block.

Nora's family was careful to implement this plan slowly. They moved from step to step as Nora showed that she was ready. They praised and supported her as she took on each new challenge. They were prepared to stop if she became uncomfortable.

Charles' family used a similar solution. They frequently offered to take him to children's shows. His answer was always a firm "No." The family accepted his response and did not pressure him. One day, a few months later, his answer surprised and delighted them. Charles sat in the last row of the theater with one parent on either side of him. He laughed a lot. He is looking forward to going to the circus when it comes to town.

An Action Plan: Empowerment

Avery's parents prolonged his bedtime ritual so that they could spend a little more time with him before he went to sleep. They told him that they would always protect him. They reassured him that there were no monsters lurking under his bed or inside his closet. He slept with a large and ferocious stuffed animal just to be sure. A new night-light was purchased for his room. Avery's parents did not fall into the trap of conducting a nightly monster search. A fruitless search fuels a child's anxieties while eroding his confidence in his parents' abilities as guardians. His bedtime behavior improved over the next several months.

Daytime Response

Steps can be taken during the day to help a fearful child. Three year olds need appropriate outlets for their aggressive feelings. They can express themselves verbally, physically, or through the creative arts.

Routines are useful. A predictable pattern to the day contributes to a sense of security.

Children's television viewing should be monitored. Cartoons, for instance, contain violent and scary material that can add to children's fears.

Fears are a normal part of growing up. Their impact can be ameliorated by parents' support and guidance.

7

TEMPERAMENT

Claude was extremely fussy about the clothes he wore. He wouldn't wear anything new until it had been washed half a dozen times. He completely rejected turtlenecks, pants with elastic waistbands, and anything made of wool. He insisted that all labels be cut out of his clothing.

Caroline was invited to a birthday party at a popular local ice-cream parlor. She had been there many times before. When she approached the door, she saw the streamers, balloons, and a vivacious group of children. She froze and refused to enter. She finally did join the party. She enthusiastically played musical chairs and hot potato. When the clown sundaes with the upside-down ice-cream cones were served, however, she broke down in a tantrum.

Claude and Caroline are children with difficult temperaments. Temperament influences the way a person approaches the world. It is useful for parents to know about temperament so that they can help their children optimally meet the challenges of growing up.

What Is Temperament?

Temperament is a collection of personality characteristics. There are nine traits that make up a child's temperament: activity level, distractability, intensity of reaction, regularity, persistence, sensory threshold, approach and withdrawal, adaptability, and mood. These characteristics combine in various ways to produce three main temperamental types: easy, slow to warm up, and difficult.

All temperamental types are normal. There is no way to predict which kind of temperament a child will have. People in the same family do not necessarily share a single temperamental style. One sibling may be difficult and the other may be easy. It is a particular challenge when parents and their children are of different temperamental types.

The Easy Child

The easy child is usually happy, accepting of new experiences, adaptable, and mildly intense. She establishes regular habits and is thus fairly predictable.

The easy child smoothly handles the challenges of being three years old. She is able to get along with children her own age. Her sunny disposition endears her to adults. She learns to share and take turns. Sometimes she wants to be the leader, and at other times she is content to follow. Her attention span is good. She enjoys both active and quiet games. Adjustment to changes, such as the start of nursery school or the birth of a sibling, go smoothly.

The Slow to Warm up Child

The slow to warm up child has a low activity level and a tendency to withdraw when presented with a new situation. She is slow to adapt and low in intensity.

Starting nursery school is a real challenge for the slow to warm up child. Even if she is prepared and eager, her initial reaction is negative. This should not be interpreted as an out-and-out rejection of school. It is a reminder that the slow to warm up child needs time to adjust to new things.

Advance planning can help her make a successful transition to school. Arrange a visit to the classroom before school starts. The child feels more comfortable if she knows what the room looks like and where materials are kept. Many schools plan a gradual phase-in for young students. This may involve several short sessions with a small number of children before the entire class comes together as a whole. Another option is to have a parent or close friend in the classroom for a few days until she becomes used to the routine.

The same kind of planning can help her with the initial awkwardness of other social encounters. Perhaps she could arrive at the birthday party a bit early and help set the table. When a playmate comes over, suggest some specific things they might do in the first uneasy minutes.

Slow to warm up children do make friends and succeed in social situations. They need the insight and acceptance that loving parents can provide.

The Difficult Child

The difficult child is a challenge. She is active and distractable. She withdraws in response to new things. The difficult child is intense and negative in mood. Body rhythms are irregular. Caroline showed a typical pattern as she changed from happy, to frightened, back to happy, and then to hysterical during the course of the party. The difficult child has a low sensory threshold. Claude demonstrated this in his extreme sensitivity to clothes. Caroline showed this in a different way when she was overwhelmed by the crowds and the noise of the party.

"Spirited" is another term used to describe these children. It is often preferred because spirited sounds so much more positive than difficult.

Parenting such a child can be difficult. The tantrums, the struggles over eating and sleeping, and the child's apparent unhappiness can be demoralizing to parents. They can feel exhausted, inadequate, and guilty. The hard times are worth it, however. These children turn out to be highly creative people with strong leadership skills.

Parents need to distinguish between temperamental and behavioral problems because they must be handled in different ways. Behavioral problems respond to limit setting and other disciplinary techniques. Temperamental problems require other coping strategies.

Claude's clothing controversies stemmed from his true temperamentally based sensitivity. Stiff, binding outfits really made him feel uncomfortable. He was not being selfish, stubborn, or willful. He was not purposely making it difficult for his family to find suitable clothes for him. Once he had clothes that felt good to him, many of the conflicts about dressing and getting out of the house in the morning disappeared.

Caroline could have been helped with the party situation. Preparation is key. She needed to be able to anticipate the smells, the noise, and the decorations. A parent sitting with her could have eased her initial entry into the party in progress. An astute parent might also have noticed when Caroline was starting to become overexcited during the games. A brief cooling-off period might have averted her tantrum over the ice-cream cones.

Difficult children also need regular discipline. They benefit from routines. They need to know what is expected of them. Rules must be enforced firmly and consistently. They respond to distraction or time-out when they are out of control. Discipline is covered in greater detail in Key 15.

A knowledge of temperament helps parents recognize their children as individuals. This understanding is key to providing sensitive, personalized, and appropriate care.

8

THE SHY CHILD

Lindsay stood by the jungle gym and watched, with her luminous gray eyes, as a tornado of activity whirled all around her. When the teacher called the group to come inside, Lindsay did not move. She allowed all the other children to pass by her before she turned and silently joined the end of the line.

Lindsay is a shy child. Shyness is a normal personality trait. It is seen in about 15% of children. Shyness may first be observed during toddlerhood. Although shyness can be identified early in life, shy children do not necessarily grow up to be shy adults.

Behavioral Characteristics

Shyness can be demonstrated in several ways. A shy child may be an observer, like Lindsay, who does not participate in activities but watches intently from the sidelines. In a social situation, a shy child may choose to play alone rather than join a group of children. She may find it difficult to make friends.

When visitors come to her home, the shy child may hide, cry, or appear nervous. In unfamiliar settings, she may cling to her parents even beyond the usually uncomfortable first 15 or 20 minutes.

A shy child may be particularly sensitive to environmental stresses. Family problems, such as marital discord, illness, death, or divorce, may be especially painful for a shy child.

The Shy Child's Needs

The shy child needs understanding, support, and empathy. Parental acceptance is paramount. Shyness is a characteristic, not a deficiency. A child does not choose to be shy, nor does she have any control over this fundamental trait. Parents sometimes pressure a reserved child because they see shyness as a liability. They worry that her needs might be overlooked, particularly in a group setting. They respond by yelling, nagging, or pushing the child into social situations. The child senses that her parents are disappointed or angry. Her self-esteem plummets.

How Parents Can Help

Parents need to value their child. Every child has positive and praiseworthy attributes. Every child is special in some way. Identifying those special characteristics is a critical part of successfully parenting a shy child.

Parents can help a shy child by building on her particular strengths. This may mean pursuing an athletic talent or a fervent interest in animals. Having an area of expertise enables a child to function in at least one domain with confidence. She feels comfortable talking with peers about a subject she knows well. Once she establishes an initial bond with other children, relationships can flourish.

Specialized knowledge can also mean distinction in the classroom. Lindsay became known as the "animal expert" of her group. As a result, she was given the responsibility of feeding the pet fish every day. This was a very visible way of acknowledging her strengths and one that conferred great status among her peers.

The Social Scene

A shy child does need extra support in social situations. New people and new situations are especially stressful. Parents should count on staying for the first few sessions of a new playgroup. The adjustment to nursery school might be eased if the child can meet one or two classmates beforehand. Seeing a few familiar faces on the first day might keep her from being overwhelmed.

A shy child may feel more comfortable in her own home. She may prefer that children visit her rather than face an unfamiliar environment. Younger children may initially prove better and less challenging playmates.

Another strategy is to provide the shy child with a gimmick. At the playground, children might gather around a child blowing bubbles. Bringing brownies when visiting a friend's house will certainly generate positive attention. These gimmicks create interest around the shy child and provide a way to bridge those first few awkward moments. The child then finds herself interacting before she has had time to become self-conscious.

Diversity makes life interesting. Not everyone can be a boisterous, life of the party type. Quiet, observant children have important roles to play, filling the ranks of the world's reporters, scientists, and writers.

9

THE ACTIVE CHILD

Zachary was a human whirlwind. One minute he'd be looking at television, and the next minute he'd be zooming his race cars around the apartment. He rarely sat down, and he never sat still. He was so fidgety he frequently fell off chairs. He was constantly touching things—the glass figurines on the display case, the stereo equipment, the contents of his mother's purse. He could climb a stack of three chairs to get to the shelf where the knives had been placed for safekeeping. Taking him to the supermarket was a nightmare. He'd knock the cans off the shelves or whine for Choco-Delight cereal. Even a short wait at the checkout line would precipitate a tantrum. Since he no longer took an afternoon nap, by dinnertime Mrs. Logan was at her wit's end.

There is a wide range to normal activity. The normal attention span for a three year old is 10 to 15 minutes. This estimate is based on an attention span of 3 to 5 minutes per year of age. A three year old should be able to sit through the reading of a simple story. He should be able to play cooperatively with peers. He should be able to carry out routine instructions.

What Is Normal Activity?

Parents need to have realistic expectations. Three year olds still need their supervision and support. Children cannot be expected to play on their own for long periods of time. They can sustain play, however, if a parent checks in with them briefly every 15 minutes or so.

Parents' own mind-sets also influence their activity tolerance. A parent who is used to handling two active children can accommodate a third with no problems. A parent who is stressed may find even a normal child's activity level unbearable.

Strategies for the Active Child

Children need physical activity every day. Take a walk, go for a jog, or ride a bicycle. In bad weather, jumping rope, jogging in place, or active dance routines are good alternatives. Children cannot and should not sit docilely in front of the television set all day. If they are not provided with appropriate ways to channel their energy, they find their own outlets. This often means using the couch as a trampoline and the dresser as a jungle gym.

Pay Attention

Sometimes provocative, impossible behavior is a plea for attention. Children quickly learn that being quiet results in their being ignored but doing something outrageous garners immediate attention. Three year olds crave attention and want as much of it as they can possibly get. They exhibit the behaviors that they know will get them the attention.

Parents must reverse this cycle by doling out attention for positive rather than negative behaviors. One way to do this is to set up an inviolate 20-minute playtime with the child once or twice a day. This time should be devoted to activities of the child's choosing. Once this routine is in place, the child knows that he has consistent access to the adult attention he wants. As a result, he is better able to tolerate the times when he must share parental attention with siblings or household chores.

Streamline

There are certain activities that drive most three year olds wild. The biggest offender is shopping. Shopping means being stimulated by colors, sounds, and people. It also means being bored, having to wait, and being physically restrained. This is not a happy combination. The best solution is to avoid shopping with the three year old. If this is impossible, make shopping trips short. Avoid going at mealtime or naptime. Bring a toy or a snack to occupy the child.

True Hyperactivity

Children who exceed the normal boundaries for activity level may have a condition called attention deficit hyperactivity disorder (ADHD). This is a neurological problem in which the brain has difficulty filtering irrelevant information and focusing on what is important. As a result, children affected by this disorder are distractable and impulsive because their attention is being pulled in many different directions at once. They never seem to be satisfied. They are moody and have sleep problems. They have difficulty following instructions, finishing tasks, and complying with routines. Children with ADHD sometimes have trouble playing with other children. Although they are eager to make friends, their aggressiveness and inability to wait their turn impede social relationships.

ADHD occurs in 3% of the population. It is six times more common in boys than in girls. This condition frequently runs in families. It is difficult to identify in young children because they are normally quite active. Sometimes it is not picked up until elementary school age, when the child is found to have difficulty paying attention in class.

Parents who are concerned that their child has ADHD should discuss this with the pediatrician. The pediatrician can observe the child and gather information from people who know him well. A referral to a neurologist or child development specialist may be made. There is no laboratory test to confirm the diagnosis. Treatment consists of training the parents in management techniques and, in certain cases, medication.

Follow-up

Zach was seen by his pediatrician, who thought that the child met the criteria for ADHD. His family was adamantly opposed to medication. The treatment focused on making Zach's environment a less overwhelming place.

Mr. and Mrs. Logan simplified Zach's room. They stored the toys he rarely played with in a closet. This way they did not have to sort out a jumble of toys at the conclusion of every day.

They made a strong effort to child-proof the house. They removed the glass figurines and other fragile objects. They installed window guards and padded the sharp edges of the furniture. They stored knives, medicines, and cleaning fluids in locked cabinets. They placed a guard on the stereo. The television and other heavy items were secured so that they could not topple over if Zach climbed on them. Once this was done, the Logans felt more relaxed. They did not have to monitor their son every minute. Their precautions ensured that Zach would not be injured even if left unsupervised.

The Logans learned that they could curb some of Zach's distractability by setting up routines. They divided each task into a set of simple steps. With practice, Zach learned what he was expected to do. In the morning, he'd get up, go to the bathroom, and dress in the clothes that had been left out the night before. His nighttime routine consisted of a bath, quiet playtime, story, and lights out. His parents were a constant presence during these transition times, encouraging him with gentle reminders and lots of praise.

41

Zachary was enrolled in a preschool. The Logans believed that a program would be a positive outlet for their son's abundant energy. They had a number of specific requirements. They looked for a program with structured activities, plenty of adult supervision, and a large playground that was used on a daily basis.

Zachary's parents wanted to learn more about ADHD. They joined a support group and did a lot of reading on their own. They learned that ADHD is a real biological entity. The child with ADHD is not distractable or impulsive on purpose. The symptoms cannot be controlled voluntarily. Zachary learned to cope with his difficulties under the guidance of his devoted and hardworking parents.

10

‧‧

THE THREE-YEAR-OLD CHECKUP

The three-year-old checkup is a time to address medical concerns, evaluate growth and development, and provide health screenings. Parents who know what to expect will be less anxious and better able to monitor their child's health care. Informed parents can also help their child by preparing her for the medical encounter. A well-prepared child is a happier, more cooperative, and less anxious patient.

The Interview

The interview focuses on updating the child's medical history. In some cases, the clinician may not have seen the child for routine care in a year. Parents must inform the practitioner of any significant illnesses, stresses, or changes in the family. This is the time to bring up any questions or concerns. To gain a complete picture of the child's functioning, the pediatrician may ask for a description of a typical day. Parents may be asked about the child's strengths and weaknesses, new skills, and progress in toilet training. Such issues as child care, work, and leisure activities can be addressed. The pediatrician also interacts with the child directly. They may play with a toy or a puppet together or chat about familiar topics, such as pets or her favorite activities.

Growth

Children assume a much leaner and more muscular look during the preschool years. Gone is the pot-bellied appearance of the typical toddler. Three year olds stand more erect, and the abdomen becomes less prominent. Fat pads on the foot recede as well, and arches can now be seen.

Weighing and measuring the child are key components of the physical examination. The physician records these measurements on a special graph called a growth chart. Using the growth chart, the physician can check to make sure that the child is maintaining a good rate of growth. The child's weight and height can also be compared with measurements of other children of the same age and sex.

Growth proceeds at a steady pace during the fourth year. The child is expected to gain between $4\frac{1}{2}$ and 5 pounds during the year. Table 10.1 lists weights for slim, average, and heavy boys and girls at age three. Children whose weights fall outside these limits should be followed closely by their doctor.

Table 10.1
WEIGHTS AT AGE THREE (POUNDS)

	Slim	Average	Heavy
Girls	$25\frac{1}{2}$	31	38
Boys	$26\frac{1}{2}$	$32\frac{1}{4}$	$39\frac{1}{4}$

Gains in height average between $2\frac{1}{2}$ and $3\frac{1}{2}$ inches during this year. By age four, the child will be about double the length she was at birth. Table 10.2, listing heights for short, average, and tall boys and girls, shows the range that can be expected at age three. Parents should discuss any concerns about their child's growth with the physician.

Table 10.2
HEIGHTS AT AGE THREE (INCHES)

	Short	*Average*	*Tall*
Girls	34¾	37	39½
Boys	35	37¼	40¼

The method by which the child's height is measured is important. By three, a child is usually measured standing up. The height is then plotted on the growth chart for 2 to 18 year olds, which is based on standing height. Baby charts (0 to 36 months) are based on a measurement taken when the baby is stretched out while lying down. Lengths on the baby chart tend to be a bit more generous (sometimes up to 1 inch) than the corresponding height on the 2- to 18-year-old chart because of the stretching. If a standing height is erroneously plotted on the baby chart, it may appear that the child is not growing well. This can cause a family needless worry. For accuracy, standing heights should be plotted on the 2- to 18-year-old chart and recumbent lengths on the baby chart.

Weight and height are also compared to each other. In most instances, weight and height should be proportional. A child who is average in weight is also expected to achieve an average height.

After 36 months, the child's head circumference is no longer measured routinely. This is because the child has already achieved over 90% of expected brain growth.

At the three-year visit the physician usually measures the child's blood pressure for the first time. This is easily accomplished if the child is given adequate preparation. The child should have a chance to try on the cuff before it is inflated. She should be told that once it is inflated it will feel tight but not painful.

45

Immunizations and Laboratory Tests

The child's primary series of immunizations and booster shots should be complete before age three. The doctor will make sure that no immunizations are missing. The next series of boosters is due before school entry. Optional tests include a blood count to look for anemia, a urine culture to look for a bladder infection, and a PPD (purified protein derivative) to look for exposure to tuberculosis.

Cholesterol screening is controversial. Some physicians favor screening everyone. Others argue against this stance because elevated childhood cholesterol levels do not always persist into adulthood. Any child with a strong family history of early heart attacks is at higher risk and should be screened. Until more information is available, the wisest course is a diet low in fat for everyone over age three. The clinician can provide specific guidelines for meeting this standard.

Vision Screening

Vision screening can be done at the three-year-old checkup even if the child cannot identify alphabet letters. There are eye charts designed for young children with pictures of common objects, such as houses, flowers, and animals. Another simple test determines whether the child is properly using both eyes to see. The physician can also check that the child's eyes are straight, not crossed. Any problems noted can then be referred to an ophthalmologist trained in the care of children.

Hearing Screening

Children need to hear clearly to develop appropriate language and academic skills. It is especially important to screen children who have had frequent middle ear infections, bacterial meningitis, head trauma, a congenital infection, mumps, or measles. Certain kinds of antibiotics (for instance, gentamicin) and diuretics can cause hearing loss. Children who have taken these medications for a prolonged period of time should have their hearing checked.

Hearing is checked by piping tones at different frequencies through a set of headphones. The child is taught to place a block in a bucket or a peg in a pegboard when she hears a sound. Some doctors have hand-held devices that accomplish the same thing without the need for headphones.

Many doctors' offices have another device, a tympanometer, which measures middle ear pressure. This device can detect signs of fluid or infection in the middle ear. It does not, however, provide information about the child's hearing.

If the doctor does not perform any direct assessment of the child's hearing, parents may be questioned about the child's response to sound. Parents should know how many words the child uses and the length of a typical sentence. They should also be able to say how clear the child's speech is to people outside the family.

If a parent has any concerns about a child's speech and language development, a formal hearing test is critical. There are specialized tests that can be performed on children unable to cooperate. No child is too young for a hearing test.

Dental Care

The three year old should have routine dental care. The pediatrician may be helpful in providing a referral to someone who has good rapport with children.

The dentist should strive to make the young patient comfortable with the sounds and sights of the office. The dentist will inspect the teeth for signs of injury, disease, or poor alignment. Cleaning, fluoride treatments, x-rays, and the application of sealants to tooth crevices are done as needed. The dentist also reviews information on brushing and flossing the teeth, nutritious foods, and the handling of dental injuries.

Preparation

At three, a visit to a health care provider need not be an ordeal. Parents can use the guidelines in this key to prepare the child for what she will encounter in the office. There are also some wonderful children's books on this topic. (See Books for Children.)

It is important for the parents to be honest if they know that the child will be having a painful procedure. It is easier for a child to learn to cope than to learn that a parent cannot be trusted. It is equally important not to use the doctor's visit as a threat. A child who is told she will get a shot if she's not good is likely to be too nervous to cooperate.

Encourage the child to bring a stuffed animal, doll, or her doctor kit along to the appointment. She and the doctor can listen to each others' heartbeats. The doctor can examine her doll's ears or take her teddy bear's blood pressure. These maneuvers can allay a child's anxiety by previewing the details of the examination. Once the child is safely home, young doctor three year old will be performing many such examinations on parents, siblings, and other members of the household.

11

~~~~~~

DAILY CARE

E quipped with their rubber ducks and their purple speckled toothbrushes, three year olds can deal with many of their own physical needs. Children feel proud and competent when they take care of themselves. It is also a great relief to parents to be able to share some of the dressing, feeding, and bathing chores.

Dressing

A three year old can dress himself almost completely. He can work a zipper and thread large buttons into buttonholes. He can put on his own jacket with the help of the flip trick. The flip trick starts with the jacket (back side down) on the floor, with the neck at the child's feet. The child bends over, inserts his hands into the sleeves, flips it over his head, and it's on.

Three year olds can put on their own shoes, but they may not always be on the correct feet. A helpful trick is to use indelible ink to draw a dot on the instep of each shoe. When the dots touch, the shoes are on properly.

Three year olds cannot tie their own shoes. Footwear with Velcro closures saves a lot of time and allows children to be independent in this area as well.

Undressing poses no problems for the typical three year old.

Eating

Three year olds should be self-sufficient in eating. They can manage a fork and spoon, although they still enjoy using their fingers at times. They are able to pour liquids from a pitcher and drink smoothly from a cup.

Grooming

A three year old can wash his own hands. Handwashing before meals and after using the toilet should be an established routine. If a child can also remember to wash his hands after coughing and sneezing, he will greatly reduce germ transmission. Liquid soap holds a particular fascination and may encourage more thorough washing. A step stool may be necessary to enable the child to reach the faucet.

Children can also do much of the washing at bathtime. They need help with shampooing, drying off, and combing their hair.

Three year olds love brushing their teeth because they consider it such a grown-up responsibility. Because their enthusiasm outweighs their skillfulness, it is suggested that the parents do the job at least once a day. It is important to brush after meals and after consuming such foods as gum, dried fruit, and caramels, which stick to the teeth and cause decay. Dentists recommend using a soft toothbrush. Children's toothpaste is tasty and attractive, and thus parents must supervise its use. A pea-sized glob is all that is necessary. Children should be taught to spit out rather than swallow the excess because too much fluoride can actually stain teeth.

Toileting

By three, 90% of children are bowel trained: 85% use the toilet for urine during the day, and 60 to 70% are dry at night.

Toilet training proceeds most smoothly when the child is developmentally ready. Signs of readiness include waking up dry in the morning and after naps, grunting, squatting, or straining after meals, being able to get to the toilet independently, being able to manipulate clothing, knowing specific words for urine and feces, and being able to follow directions. If the child is not ready, ignore all pressure from neighbors, in-laws, and magazines. Toilet training can never be started too late, but it can be started too early. It is better to put off training until stressful events, such as the birth of a new baby or a move, have resolved.

Most children start with a potty chair. Other families may choose to use the toilet right away. If the child is going to use the regular toilet, a stool placed nearby allows him to climb up independently. It also provides needed support for his dangling legs. Have the child sit on the chair with his clothes on just to get used to it. Reading him a story is a way of getting him to spend time there voluntarily.

The next step is to have the child sit on the potty with his clothes off in the early morning or after a meal, when he is likely to need the toilet. Praise him if he eliminates in the toilet. If he is not successful, remember that there will be plenty of other opportunities. If the child has a bowel movement in his diaper, empty it into the potty to demonstrate where the feces belong. If family members feel comfortable, have the child accompany them to the bathroom. Using the toilet like everyone else is a powerful motivator for a young child.

The child initially needs help wiping himself. Girls should wipe from front to back to avoid introducing germs from the anus into the vagina. Remind the child to wash his hands after using the toilet. It is not unusual for a child to be afraid to flush the toilet. Parents may have to assume this chore at the beginning.

Learning to use the toilet is a complicated process. Accidents and setbacks, particularly during times of stress, are common. It is important never to ridicule or punish the child for toileting accidents.

It is really a marvel to watch a three year old put on his own clothes or brush his teeth. The job may be imperfect or take a long time to complete, but there is a real thrill attached to the statement, "I did it myself!"

12

~~~~~~

FEEDING AND NUTRITION

Simone refused to eat any food that was not red. Mrs. Bloomingdale quickly learned to make liberal use of tomato sauce, catsup, and strawberry preserves.

Brett ate nothing but pizza, morning, noon, and night, for three months straight. Then one day he refused even to look at a slice. His parents organized a neighborhood pizza party to dispose of the vast stores that remained in their freezer.

Jeremy's eating pattern was a puzzle to his parents. Most days he ate only one meal, yet some days he displayed a voracious appetite. On those days he would complain that he was starving even after eating three solid meals and two snacks.

Feeding a three year old can present some interesting challenges.

Requirements

Children in this age group require between 1,000 and 1,600 calories per day to grow well. Meeting this requirement is not difficult. One fabulous ice-cream sundae with toppings, whipped cream, nuts, and chocolate sprinkles will do it. The challenge is to meet the caloric goal in a healthy way and establish good eating patterns for a lifetime. The latest nutritional information shows benefits from a diet that emphasizes fruits, vegetables, and grains and minimizes red meat and fats. Table 12.1 outlines the specifics of this kind of diet.

Table 12.1
FOODS FOR THE THREE TO FOUR YEAR OLD

Food Group	Number of Servings/Day	Serving Size
Milk and cheese	4	½ to ¾ cup
Meat	3	1 egg
		3 Tb lean meat
		1½ Tb peanut butter
Fruits, vegetables	4 or more	½ c citrus juice
		4 Tb vegetable
		½ cup apple
Cereals	4	1 slice toast
		1 oz cereal
		½ c macaroni
Fats	1	1 Tb
Sweets	1½ portions	1 portion =
		⅓ c pudding
		⅓ c ice cream
		2 3-inch cookies
		2 Tb jelly

Parents should make sure that the child's diet contains adequate amounts of iron, zinc, and calcium. Good sources for iron include beef, liver, cereals, and wheat germ. Zinc can be obtained from red meat, seafood, cereals, and legumes, such as peas and beans. Calcium can be found in milk and dairy foods, such as cheese and yogurt. Powdered milk can be added to soups and puddings if a child does not like milk.

Fiber is necessary in a child's diet. A high-fiber diet is associated with a reduced risk of cancer of the colon. Fiber can be obtained from vegetables, which also provide vitamin A, and whole grains.

Limits should be placed on cholesterol, salt, and sweets. The fatty plaques that are the basis of heart disease start forming at an early age. A low-fat diet is prudent for children three years old and above. Increased salt consumption can lead to high blood pressure in susceptible individuals. Children acquire a taste for salty foods by being exposed to them. Foods to be avoided include snack foods, canned soup, canned spaghetti, and luncheon meats. Sweets that are in prolonged contact with the teeth promote tooth decay. Classic offenders include lollipops and caramels.

Tines and Times

By age three children are generally quite self-sufficient when it comes to feeding. They can drink from a cup. They can manage a fork and spoon by themselves. There may be times when they may revert to eating with their fingers. Encouragement and adult modeling of utensil usage should keep them on track. An adult should continue to cut foods that require the use of a sharp knife.

The mealtime schedule includes the three major meals, as well as midmorning and midafternoon snacks. Children love snacks and often need the energy boost they provide. Snacks should be culled from the list of recommended foods in Table 12.1. Raw vegetable sticks with a yogurt-based dip, fruit, fruit juice, and crackers are good choices. Frozen treats can be made from fruit juice or yogurt/fruit combinations.

Is My Child Getting Enough?

Many parents worry that their child is not eating enough. It is important to remember the distinction between an adult-sized portion and a portion suitable for a three year old. A portion of chicken for a three year old is 2 ounces; 4 ounces of milk is considered a portion, as is one slice of toast. With these portion sizes in mind, it is easy to see how a child who eats "nothing" all day can easily meet his daily caloric requirement.

The Clean Plate Syndrome

It is important not to push children into overeating. Overeating can lead to obesity. Obese children often have low self-esteem and poor peer relationships. As a result, they tend to isolate themselves and become physically inactive. This leads to a worsening of the obesity. Obesity is linked to serious medical problems in adulthood, including diabetes, high blood pressure, and heart disease. Children should be allowed to stop eating when they feel full rather than when the plate is clean.

Eat to Grow

Children at this age need to learn the right reasons to eat. They should know that they eat to grow. Food should not be used as a reward for good behavior. Adhering to this rule prevents eating from getting mixed up with emotional issues, such as approval and affection.

Food should not be used as a pacifier. Children sometimes ask for something to eat when they are bored or in need of attention. Giving them food at these times confuses the issue of eating to grow with the habit of eating just to pass the time.

TV Dinners

Eating while watching television is not recommended as a general practice. Children become so engrossed in the show that they do not really pay attention to the quantity of food they are consuming. Extra calories and inactivity are the recipe for obesity.

Television is also not helpful for the reluctant eater. Parents sometimes think that amusing the child during meals will lead to greater food consumption. Watching television during meals usually ends up distracting the child and actually causes him to eat less. A more optimal approach is to determine why the child has an eating problem and address it directly.

Even the company of Inspector Gadget is no substitute for the family around the dinner table. Eating is a social experience as well as a way of providing fuel for the body. Families should make sitting down together for a meal a daily priority. This is a time to catch up on everyone's news, share ideas, and establish traditions. A child's table manners can be improved by parental modeling of appropriate behavior. A child who is reluctant to try new foods may be more amenable after seeing asparagus on a parent's plate.

The Potato Chip Monster and Other Influences

Television also profoundly influences children's food choices. Many children's shows are sponsored by manufacturers of salty snack foods, sugary cereals, soft drinks, and other high-calorie, low-nutrient foods. Children want to have the foods that are endorsed by their favorite characters. Healthy foods lack the charisma of their heavily advertised junk food counterparts.

Children also have an impact on each other's intake. Cameron wouldn't even look at chicken at home but ate three pieces when he visited Camille's house. Julie loved her mother's carrot soup but stopped eating it after a friend pronounced it "yucky."

Parents in these situations must be flexible. Cameron's father got the recipe and added chicken á la Camille to the family's menu. Julie's mother put the carrot soup on the back burner for a few months and served carrot sticks with yogurt dip instead.

Fast Food

One of the first symbols a child seems to recognize is the logo for one of the ubiquitous hamburger chains. He notices it on bus rides and walks in the neighborhood. He sees the signs on the highway and the billboards in the subway. The appeal from the child's point of view is the stimulating atmosphere and the toys that come with the food. Parents are lured by the quick service and the knowledge that the meal will be eaten without complaint.

What is a parent to do? There is a range of options regarding fast food. One is to ban it altogether as nutritionally incorrect. Another is to reserve it for special occasions. Some families make a ritual of going after a visit to the pediatrician or on the child's birthday.

Many of the chains have responded to the public by attempting to reduce the salt and fat content of the food and broaden their menus. Families concerned about nutrition can patronize these restaurants if they are willing to limit their selections. Parents must make clear which foods will be permitted. This is not a workable compromise, however, for the child who will only accept the traditional burger, fries, and milkshake.

Restaurant Meals

It is not impossible to eat in a real restaurant with a three year old. Some children may even rise to the occasion and display a special sense of decorum.

There are some precautions to be taken, however. Do not take a child out to eat when he is already ravenous. The food cannot possibly be served fast enough, and the child will turn irritable and cranky.

Choose a restaurant that prepares food simply or has a children's menu. Check the menu in advance to make sure that they are serving something the child likes. Consider ordering an appetizer-sized portion for the child, or let him select his meal from the adults' plates. In any case, he will be better company if he is happy with his food.

Waiting time must be kept to a minimum. It would be better to eat early than to arrive at the height of the dinner rush. Bring crayons and paper, a book, or a small windup toy to amuse the child while waiting for the food to arrive. Munching on crackers or bread can also make the wait less tedious.

Dining companions must recognize that the child is unlikely to linger over his food, savoring each morsel. Someone from the group should be prepared to walk the child around the block when he gets restless. Bon appetit!

Picky Eaters

Three year olds want to be able to control some aspect of their lives. Picky eating is one way of exercising control.

It is important not to make the child's eating pattern a major battleground. If directly confronted, the three year old's pride leaves him no recourse but to stand his ground. If he really feels pressured, he may refuse to eat altogether.

One way to defuse eating problems is to give the three year old some voice in meal planning. The trick is to offer a choice between two acceptable alternatives.

A child is less likely to reject foods that he has had a hand in creating. A child can assist in the kitchen by pouring, mixing, or sifting ingredients. He can be given his own piece of dough to knead and shape. Brett may try his first bran muffin only because he helped to make it. Making healthy foods together sets a powerful example for a child.

Uneven appetites, like Jeremy's, are normal and common at three. Children are no longer growing as fast as they did during infancy, so that a massive daily influx of calories is not necessary. Appetite is influenced by physical growth, activity, and health status. It is wise to allow children to respond to their bodies' cues by matching their intake to their appetite.

Follow-up

Simone's and Brett's parents recognized that they were two supremely picky eaters.

Simone's mother coped by providing a nutritionally, although not esthetically, diverse menu. From time to time, she gently offered foods of different colors. Brett's parents recognized that food jags are quite common in this age group. Both situations resolved on their own because the children became bored with their rigid eating patterns.

Jeremy's parents were reassured by the pediatrician that their son was growing well. Adding a daily vitamin supplement to his diet put their fears to rest.

13

SLEEP

Mr. and Mrs. Ames were clearing the last of the dinner dishes when they heard a familiar voice call out, "Mom, Dad, I need another good night kiss." That request satisfied, the Ames' returned to their task. "Mom, Dad, I'm dying of thirst. I need a drink of water." Ben followed up with complaints that his room was too dark, his blanket was too hot, his pillow was not sufficiently fluffy, and there were monsters behind the curtains. Then he needed an escort to the bathroom and someone to look for his missing teddy bear. Mr. and Mrs. Ames thought he was finally asleep until a sweetly smiling child appeared in the kitchen inquiring, "Do you need any company?" "Benjamin! That's it!" his mother shouted. "We're all going to bed." Ben happily trotted off to bed as all activity in the household ceased.

Sleep serves a critical function in replenishing children's energy stores. Three year olds, however, view sleep from a totally different perspective. They consider sleep an annoying intrusion on their important activities. This key highlights ways that parents can avert bedtime battles and make going to sleep a more pleasant family experience.

Sleep Schedules

Typical three year olds require between 11 and 12 hours of sleep per day. Some children sleep the entire allotment at night; others still take an afternoon nap.

The timing of the afternoon nap is critical. Late or long afternoon naps can complicate the daily schedule. Children need four to six hours of waking time after a nap before they are tired enough to return to sleep. If the afternoon nap goes too late, they will not be sleepy at a reasonable bedtime. If they sleep a long time during the day, they have a reduced requirement for sleep at night.

Most three year olds would benefit from some quiet time in the afternoon even if they do not actually sleep. A video nap is one option. Set the children up with an entertaining, nonviolent videotape for half an hour. This time is particularly enjoyable if the parent is nearby reading, doing some paperwork, or even resting.

Another way to make quiet time special is to designate some special toys that can be played with only at that time. Good choices include puzzles, markers and paper, blocks, and figurines. Reading books and listening to music are also excellent quiet activities.

Bedtime Blues

The three year old resists going to bed because it means leaving the excitement of his waking life. The early evening schedule should feature low-key activities. The idea is to have fun while helping the child wind down from the fast pace of the day. Reading and playing board games are good options. Roughhousing or scary videos should be left for another time.

Teach the child to recognize his bedtime on the clock. This makes bedtime a reality, not some arbitrary parental idea. As the time draws near, set a kitchen timer to alert the child about how much playtime remains. This arrangement frees the parents from the chore of nagging about bedtime. A timer increases compliance and reduces pleas for "just five more minutes." The child knows it is futile to beg a timer for leniency.

When he complies, this is a perfect time to reward the child with praise or a hug.

Some children are motivated by bedtime sticker charts. Children earn a sticker for each night they go to bed without a fuss. Parents can even increase the stakes by offering a special treat for five stickers in a row. Three year olds like the concrete evidence of their good behavior and work hard to avoid the reproach of a blank and stickerless space.

Bedtime Ritual

The bedtime ritual is still important, and 20 to 30 minutes should be set aside for a calm and loving transition to sleep. It is ideal if both parents can participate. Then the child is not distracted by what he thinks are more interesting-sounding activities taking place in another part of the house.

The particular format of the ritual is unique to the family. Reading books, recapping the day's events, or listening to music are popular choices. Allow the child to exercise some autonomy by choosing the music or the book. Parents should clearly state in advance how many books will be read to avert tantrums or begging for "just one more story."

Nightmares

Nightmares are normal and common in this age group. Nightmares are nothing more than bad dreams. They occur as the child processes his daytime experiences during dreaming sleep. A three year old's nightmares are populated by scary animals or imaginary creatures. These beings symbolize the aggression he is struggling to master in his daily life. The plot of the nightmare often involves the child being lost or chased.

A child who has had a bad dream needs comfort and empathy. He will benefit from a hug or some quiet talk until he feels ready to go back to bed. Reassure him that he is safe. It is useful to remind him that the dream was not real. It was only a story inside his head. It is important to remember that although the events depicted in the nightmare are imaginary, the scary feelings they produce are quite real.

Monsters

Worries surface at bedtime as the distractions of the day fade from center stage. Three year olds worry about real things in their lives, such as school, siblings, and toilet training. Vivid three-year-old imaginations also contribute things to fear, such as monsters under the bed or ghosts behind the curtains.

Parents need to emphasize, as part of the bedtime ritual, their roles as protectors of their children. Positive interventions that leave the children feeling more capable and in control are helpful. Monster spray (a plastic atomizer containing colored water) can be left at the bedside for protection. A ferocious stuffed animal can be chosen to stand guard.

An exhaustive search of the room that turns up no monster, however, can be more frightening than reassuring. The child then concludes that the monster is so devious that it can even outsmart his brilliant parents. A quick glance under the bed or behind the curtains is sufficient to demonstrate a belief in the child's story and a commitment to protect him.

Three year olds need to sleep at night so that they can learn and grow during the day. These guidelines will help parents meet their children's requirements for sleep.

14

PLAY

Jocelyn: "I'll be the dog and you can be my owner."

Kendra: "OK, doggie, I'm taking you for a walk."

Jocelyn: "I love you, owner."

Kendra: "I'm glad I picked you from the pet shop." (Picks up a block.) "Here is a treat for you."

Play has a central importance in the lives of three year olds. Through play, children express ideas and feelings, develop social relationships, and understand their world.

Play at three is considerably more sophisticated than it was at two. Three year olds play cooperatively rather than side by side. Compromise, bargaining, and negotiation are now a part of their interaction.

Symbolic Play

Three year olds are capable of symbolic play. In symbolic play, one object can stand in for another. A blue rug can represent a pond and a stick can be the fishing pole. A block can be a dog's bone or a sandwich. Realistic toys are no longer necessary for play to be sustained.

Play as Learning

Three year olds explore fundamental themes in their play. Jocelyn and Kendra's play involved the concept of nurturance. Belonging and caring are very central to the lives of three year olds. The owner-pet scenario is a safe context in which to explore these powerful emotions.

Children learn essential social skills as they play. For Jocelyn and Kendra's play to proceed, they had to agree on their role assignments. They also both accepted a modification of reality in which dogs talk. Three year olds' ability to cooperate makes this kind of play possible. They even find ways to resolve conflicts so that the play can continue. Three year olds tend not to hoard or fight over toys. At this age girls and boys are still playing together.

Dramatic Play

Play helps a child understand both the scary and mundane aspects of her world. A child who has recently been to the pediatrician may choose to play doctor. In her play, however, she assumes the role of the physician and gives rather than receives the shots. A child whose parent recently returned to work may enact scenes of leave-taking over and over. Repetitive play helps a child adjust to a new or stressful situation. A three year old also enjoys playing out everyday experiences, such as going to the store or taking the bus. The child dramatizes her observations and comes away with a better understanding of how the world works.

Play also helps children learn about societal roles. Children cast their pretend dramas with mothers, fathers, teachers, doctors, firefighters, and animals. They try on new parts. What does it feel like to be the mother? How do I like being the teacher? They match their view of the world with others. Can girls be doctors? Can boys be teachers? Their imaginations stretch to allow them to act as animals or babies. They can handle multiple roles. One child can be the wife and mother and even the voice of the baby.

Other Kinds of Play

Three year olds engage in practice play and constructive play. Practice play involves working on new skills. New skills important to three year olds include motor skills, such as throwing a ball or stringing beads. Constructive play means making things. Painting a picture and building a tower with blocks are examples of constructive play. Interesting sex differences have been noted in children's block play. Girls and boys use blocks in distinct ways. Girls use blocks to build enclosures for animals or human figures, and boys use blocks to build towers.

Board Games

Three year olds are beginning to be ready for simple board games. These games provide practice in following rules, manipulating small tokens, recognizing colors, and counting. Children learn to be patient and take turns. This is also a good time to introduce the concepts of good sportsmanship and playing for fun.

Most of these games rely on luck rather than skill. Children have an opportunity to handle mild frustration when they lose. They can also learn to be gracious rather than gloating when they win.

Parents and Play

Parents can help their children become good players. This is important because children who are good players are popular with their peers. Teach children to initiate play by asking another child, "Would you like to play with me?" If another child is playing with a toy she wants, have her ask, "Can I play with that when you're done?" or "Can I have that next?"

Parents don't need to get involved every time children have a conflict during play. Disagreeing gives them a chance to learn to reason, defend a position, and become more independent. The only exception might be when a child is excluded from play. In school, there is usually an official policy prohibiting exclusion. At home, the excluded party is often a younger sibling. Parents must judge the appropriateness of including a younger child in the three year olds' play. A small child may come in handy if they are playing house but may be a nuisance if block play is on the agenda.

A three year old also enjoys playing with her parents. It means a lot to a child when the parents set aside their work and focus on an activity of her choosing. Parents must remember not to take over the play. They should allow the child to take the lead in assigning roles and suggesting the scenario. If the block tower is toppling, they can suggest a solution rather than jump in and fix it. The child needs to develop confidence in her own ability to solve problems.

Independent Play

Children also need to develop the ability to amuse themselves in solitary play. Three year olds can be expected to play alone for 10 to 15 minutes.

The best way to start is to have the child and the adult engage in an activity together. After play has been established, the adult should excuse herself briefly and then return. The adult's absences can gradually be increased in length until the child is maintaining solitary play for 10 minutes. The duration of independent play can be sustained for longer than 10 minutes if the adult checks in periodically. Even a nonverbal gesture, such as a touch on the shoulder, indicates to the child that she is not being ignored.

Play is an important pastime for children. Three year olds play with a special vitality and passion.

15

DISCIPLINE

Dustin dismantled his father's alarm clock.

Laurel lit her uncle's cigarette lighter and ignited a piece of paper.

Ryan removed a carton of eggs from the refrigerator. He broke open a dozen eggs directly onto the kitchen floor.

M ost parents would agree that each of these scenarios calls for disciplinary action, but they may not agree about exactly what to do. Would it be best to yell, place the child in time-out, or deliver a sharp smack to the buttocks?

There is more to discipline than punitive action in response to a transgression. The term "discipline" comes from the Greek word for teaching. Discipline means teaching children appropriate behavior. Young children cannot monitor their behavior and control their impulses. They need adults to guide them.

Children need limits. Three year olds find it scary to be allowed to run free. Children understand that limits are a form of protection set forth by caring parents. Even as they challenge some limits, they learn to accept others. This is part of the cycle of growing up.

The tools for discipline include hugs, kisses, praise, explanations, limit setting, and modeling appropriate behavior. These elements are all used to underscore desired behavior.

Punishment, in contrast, has a much more limited usefulness. Punishment tells children what they ought not do. It does not leave them a clue about how they should behave the next time.

Consider Their Motives

All children do things that are destructive, dangerous, or annoying, but this is rarely their primary intent. Children's undesirable behaviors are often innocent by-products of their explorations.

Dustin took the clock apart because he was fascinated by mechanical equipment. He had no idea that he would not be able to put it back together.

Laurel was emulating her beloved uncle when she used the lighter. She did not anticipate how quickly the paper would go up in flames or how much damage it would cause.

Ryan was being a scientist. He systematically examined every egg to find out whether each contained a white and a yolk.

If, however, a child's actions are consistently hostile or destructive, the pediatrician should be consulted for help.

Positive Discipline in Action

The central idea in positive discipline is to learn from the incident and set up a system to prevent it from happening again. Dustin's and Laurel's families responded by placing all fragile and dangerous objects out of the children's reach. They reinforced the idea that the children were not allowed to touch others' possessions without permission. Ryan's family set up a rule prohibiting him from opening the refrigerator without an adult present.

The families were still aggravated about cleaning up the messes and having to throw out the broken clock, but they realized that their anger was not productive. Anger was not going to teach their children appropriate behavior. Anger was not the right response to innocent curiosity.

Negative Discipline in Action

It is easy to see how Dustin's, Laurel's, or Ryan's actions could provoke a torrent of parental anger. ("Look what you've done. You are such a brat. I hate you.") Some parents might be so angry that they'd lash out physically at the child.

Verbal put-downs and corporal punishment are not productive in the long run. Although the parent may be temporarily relieved by an expression of anger, this accomplishes little for the child. He feels bad that his parent is upset, but he does not know what he has done wrong. Was exploring wrong? Was being curious wrong? Or was it touching someone else's things? He has not been helped to find a way to avoid making this same mistake in the future.

There are other negative consequences to this approach. Shaming or yelling at a child erodes his self-esteem. The parent did not label his behavior as bad. The parent clearly stated that *he* was bad. If the child feels that he's already a bad person, there is no point in trying to improve his behavior. Hitting a child sends the message that it is acceptable to resolve conflicts by physical means. The child now feels entitled to use physical force when he disagrees with other people.

Setting Limits

Positive discipline does not mean merely setting up rules after the fact. Limits are needed proactively to keep the household running smoothly.

Rules should be stated clearly and specifically. (All passengers in the car must wear seat belts.)

71

Rules must be enforced consistently. If the child knows he has to fasten his seat belt on every trip, he submits without a fuss. If he knows he only has to buckle up sometimes, he will challenge the seat belt rule on every trip. He will want to establish whether it is a seat belt or a non-seat belt trip.

Rules need to be explained. (Everybody in the car wears seat belts because they keep us safe.) Parents usually have good reasons for the rules they set up. Three year olds are just beginning to respond to reason. This is an excellent time to get into the habit of explaining. Letting children know the rationale behind the rules makes them seem less arbitrary and mean-spirited.

Rules must be appropriate to the child's developmental level. It is not fair, for instance, to punish a young child for lying or for less than perfect behavior in the supermarket. These standards are beyond the capability of a three year old.

Rules should be kept to a manageable and realistic number. Not every aspect of life with a three year old can be regulated. The priorities should be keeping the child safe and helping him learn to respect the rights of others. Minor, non-dangerous behaviors, such as whining and showing off, can be safely ignored. Once the child realizes that he does not get attention for these behaviors, they will stop.

Some parents don't set limits. They may have given up because it is so difficult to enforce rules firmly and consistently. Others offer the excuse that rules impinge on a child's creativity. Such a decision has severe repercussions for a child. A child without limits is spoiled. He always wants his own way and finds it hard to get along with others. As a result, he is unhappy and unpopular.

Avoiding Conflict

There are scores of potential daily conflicts with a three year old. Parents can save energy by anticipating, avoiding, and averting some kinds of conflicts.

Child-proofing the home anticipates conflicts. Removing fragile and dangerous objects eliminates the need to say "No, don't touch it, put it down," endlessly throughout the day.

Parents should recognize "no-win" situations, such as battling with a child about eating. Eating is an area in which the child has ultimate control. Pressuring him only increases his resistance. A better approach is to praise him when he eats well and ignore the other times.

Distraction is also a useful technique. In the supermarket, furnishing the child with a snack to eat or a toy to play with keeps him from running away, throwing cans from the shelves, or adding unwanted items to the shopping cart.

Logical Consequences

In certain circumstances, three year olds can learn from the natural consequences of their misbehavior. If they write on the walls, the crayons are taken away. If they throw the shape sorter and it breaks, it is not replaced. This strategy is only appropriate for three year olds if breaking the rules does not prove physically harmful to them. It is not appropriate, for instance, to let a three year old find out for himself why children must hold an adult's hand while crossing the street. This would be an extremely costly lesson.

Positive Reinforcement

Children thrive on hugs, kisses, praise, and positive attention. They shape their behavior to obtain these reactions. They dislike it when attention is withdrawn. They react by stopping behaviors that are ignored. The lessons for parents are clear: Pay attention to desirable behavior, and ignore unwanted behavior.

Children need to hear positive messages. Positive messages should outnumber negative messages on a daily basis. It is instructive for parents to spend some time listening to what they say to children. They may be surprised how often they hear themselves saying, "Don't do that. Stop it. No, no, no."

To change the balance, parents need to notice the child being good at least 20 times a day. Look for him playing quietly with a toy or watching a video. Go over and place a hand on his shoulder, or blow him a kiss, or say, "I like the way you are playing with the blocks." The positive reinforcement can be quick and is not intended to interrupt his concentration. It is merely an acknowledgment that the child's appropriate behavior is noticed.

Frequent praise is also important. Praise is a way of communicating expectations and values. Specific positive messages are more helpful to the child than global praise. "I like the way you shared the toy" tells him more than "You're a good boy." With the first statement, he understands the desired behavior and can work to replicate it. Praise also builds self-esteem. A child with high self-esteem can better withstand criticism because he understands that it is directed at his behavior and not at him personally.

Parents must be conscious of their behavior and set a good example. Children notice and copy their parents' behavior. If the parent yells, so does the child. If the parent hits, the child sees this as acceptable behavior.

Time-out

Time-out is the classic tool of positive discipline. It can be used as often as necessary. It carries no risk of emotional harm. It is the perfect example of adult restraint in action. It gives both parent and child a chance to calm down and avoid escalation of the conflict. Time-out is effective with such problems as aggressive behavior and not following directions.

The methodology is very simple. When a time-out is needed, start by calmly stating the rule that was broken. This, of course, must be a rule that was previously known to the child. ("Ryan, you are not allowed to go to the refrigerator by yourself. Time-out.") It is important to act immediately so that the child makes the association between the rule being broken and the time-out.

Walk or carry the child to the designated time-out location. It should be a boring, safe place away from the main activity areas. Time-out is not a punishment, so the place should not be dark or scary. Because it should be a place with few distractions, the child's room is not a particularly good choice. A heavy chair placed in a hallway is an appropriate site.

Three minutes is a reasonable time-out interval for a three year old. Set a kitchen timer to keep track of the time. Do not talk to the child while he's in time-out. He should be spending the time focusing on calming himself. If he gets up before the interval has elapsed, return him to time-out.

Time-out is successfully completed if the child has remained in the chair for the alloted period. A three year old will probably not sit quietly for the entire time but should at least be calmer than he was at the outset. If the child is still hysterical when the bell rings, reset it for an additional minute. Remind the child, "You can leave time-out when you are calm."

After the time-out, the child returns with a clean slate. There should be no criticism or rehashing of the incident that led to the time-out.

Time-out works because children hate to have their play interrupted and attention withdrawn. Removed from the inciting situation, it is easier to calm down and regain control.

Parents also need a plan of action that works in public places. Children quickly learn to exploit the situation if they are not disciplined outside the home. A corner of a store, a bench in a mall, or a building lobby can serve as time-out spots.

Direct Confrontation
There are times when a problem must be handled more directly. A child at the sandbox, for instance, may have to relinquish a borrowed toy to a departing playmate.

Get down to the child's eye level, make eye contact, and say, "Jasmine, Allison has to go home now. Please give her back the shovel." If there is no response, ask again in a firmer voice. If there is still no action, physically help her hand over the object. If this resolves the situation, say nothing further about it. If Jasmine snatches the shovel back or hits Allison, a time-out is needed.

Discipline is more than blind obedience. Young children need patient and loving teaching to become self-disciplined adults.

16

TANTRUMS

"I can't do it," screamed Rachel. She flung her arms out and knocked over the block tower she had been building. Her three-year-old fingers could not get the small cubes to conform exactly to her architectural plans. She picked up a handful of blocks and threw them against the wall. Then she stomped furiously on the remaining blocks. It looked as if she were trying to drive the blocks right through the planks on the floor.

Justin and his mother approached the checkout counter at the Big A supermarket after a long morning of shopping. "I want that," he announced loudly, pointing to a fat pink package of Super Luscious bubble gum. Mrs. Reilly quietly reminded her son that bubble gum is not a healthy food. "But I waaant it," Justin replied in a louder and more shrill voice. He began to cry and kick his legs. Mrs. Reilly offered him a pretzel. The pretzel was knocked to the floor by one of Justin's flailing limbs. His face was pink and tearstained, his red hair matted down with perspiration. Mrs. Reilly felt the eyes of every Big A customer upon her. Surely they were enjoying this real-life drama far more than the offerings of the check-out line gossip magazines.

Three year olds are in their last year of eligibility for tantrums. Parents can expect to see fewer tantrums during the fourth year.

What Are Tantrums?

Tantrums are an expression of frustration. An adult is expected to channel frustration through verbal means. An adult can yell at the inconsiderate driver who cut her off on the highway. A blistering letter can be written to a company whose stockings always tear on the first wearing. Children, whose use of language is still imprecise and unsatisfying, continue to rely on physical means to convey their point of view. This is particularly true in a crisis. The result is the crying, kicking, pounding, screaming compendium known as a tantrum.

Preventing Tantrums

The ideal way to deal with tantrums is to prevent them. Parents know which situations are likely to lead to conflicts. Creative advance planning can avert at least some tantrums.

Bring an acceptable snack to the supermarket so that the child is less tempted by junk food. There are supermarkets with checkout lines free of candy and gum. At the playground, a five-minute warning before it's time to leave provides the child with a chance to wrap up his game. Some situations should be avoided altogether. Most three year olds are not sufficiently altruistic to go to the toy store solely to buy a present for someone else.

Two Kinds of Tantrums

There are actually two kinds of tantrums: the exasperation tantrum and the manipulative tantrum. They have different causes and require different responses.

The Exasperation Tantrum

Rachel's is an example of the exasperation tantrum. She started out happily building a complicated structure with blocks. As frequently happens at this age, her ideas outstripped her abilities. When she could not get her hands to perform up to her specifications, she became enraged. A three year old's rather concrete way of dealing with disappointment is to try to obliterate its source. This is what Rachel did. She destroyed the building and even tried to pulverize the blocks themselves. She needed to get rid of the symbols of her failure.

The Manipulative Tantrum

The manipulative tantrum is quite different. Manipulative tantrums occur in the context of a battle of wills between caretaker and child. For instance, the parent says it's time to leave the park, and the child says no. Another setup is the child who wants ice cream before dinner and the parent who doesn't think this is a reasonable idea.

Manipulative tantrums evolve from healthy developmental advances. The three year old is proud of his desires, beliefs, and ideas. He seeks to defend them in his interactions with adults. There are times when his ability to express himself verbally is overwhelmed. Energetic and persistent crying, kicking, and screaming take the place of eloquent words. This is how Justin made sure that his mother understood how desperately he wanted the gum.

Handling the Exasperation Tantrum

It is easy to be sympathetic to a child who is frustrated by her inability to accomplish a particular task. "It's really hard to get the blocks to go where you want them to sometimes," responded Rachel's nursery school teacher, Mr. Grooms, when he heard the ruckus. Mr. Grooms enveloped Rachel in a tight hug until her sobs subsided. "How about if you help me get the juice for snack?" he asked. Rachel smiled and nodded and the two of them trotted off hand in hand.

Rachel's teacher managed the situation in an optimal way. He gave Rachel the verbal comfort of his words and the physical comfort of his arms. He did not dwell on her failure. No lecture was given on the proper handling of blocks. Mr. Grooms did not offer to help Rachel rebuild because he understood that she wanted nothing further to do with blocks for awhile.

After Rachel was calm, Mr. Grooms still kept her close. He engaged her in a special task that would restore her sense of competence. Later in the day there would be time to clean up the mess in the block corner.

Handling the Manipulative Tantrum

Handling the manipulative tantrum is a bit trickier. The most important thing is for the adult to remain calm. This is a challenge because the adult juggles her own emotions of anger or embarrassment in addition to handling an out-of-control child.

What upsets some parents is the child's lack of compliance. The do-it-because-I-say-so approach clashes with a three year old's growing self-confidence. More subtle ways of dealing with conflicts must be developed. Good solutions accommodate both the parents' greater experience and the child's emerging spirit.

The first step is to figure out which phase of the tantrum the child is in. If the tantrum is just starting to build up, distraction can be tried. Something really silly may shift the child's focus. "Wow, I think I see Big Bird ducking down the juice aisle. Let's go and catch up with him."

Once the tantrum is in full swing, it is too late for distraction. Justin was so worked up by the time his mother tried the distraction with a pretzel gambit that he didn't even notice it. At this point, the most effective strategy is to ignore the tantrum while making sure that the child remains safe. Once the child realizes that he is not being very persuasive, he will stop.

Ignoring a tantrum can be difficult. Try to imagine a serene idyll far from the tumultuous aisles of the Big A supermarket. It is important to remember that the onlookers staring the hardest are those reliving their own similar experiences.

Another strategy is to remove the child from the tantrum-provoking stimulus. The child calms down when he realizes that he will not be getting his way. This is particularly useful for the tantrum in the toy store. It is highly impractical, however, for the supermarket tantrum. Any parent who has just spent an hour gathering groceries is not going to abandon them at the checkout counter.

Sometimes a parent hits a child, believing that this will shock him out of the tantrum state. A parent may also hit a child out of anger. A blow merely refuels the tantrum. It frightens the out-of-control child to see his parent out of control. The result is that he cries even more. It is also counterproductive. The child needs to learn how to resolve conflicts through verbal rather than physical means. A parent needs to model appropriate behavior for the child.

Giving the child what he wants is also a temptation. "After all," thought Mrs. Reilly, "What's one pack of gum?" Parents should be aware of the message that this action conveys to the child. It shows the child that tantrums get him what he wants. It guarantees that the child continues to use tantrums as a tactic.

Finishing Touches

Mrs. Reilly needed the groceries, so she had no choice but to endure the tantrum. She imagined a favorite scene. She was drifting in a rowboat on Lake Onota feeling the warm sun on her face as she watched the puffy white clouds glide by.

Justin soon exhausted his supply of tears. He took a deep breath and expelled one last sputtering sob. He looked up at his mother cautiously, waiting for her reaction. Mrs. Reilly knelt down and put her arms around her son. "I love you but I didn't like what you did in there," she whispered. "Let's go home now."

Mrs. Reilly aptly handled the tantrum aftermath. She knew that Justin needed reassurance that their relationship had not been irreparably damaged. She gave him support while making it clear that she did not condone his behavior. There was no reason to be spiteful or hold a grudge. The incident was over. They had left the store without buying gum. Mrs. Reilly had prevailed.

Tantrums are on the wane in the fourth year. These once awesome displays will soon be only a relic of babyhood.

17

BEHAVIOR PROBLEMS

P arents of three year olds typically have many concerns about their behavior. This key looks at ways to cope with some of the most common issues.

Bedwetting (Enuresis)

A significant number of three year olds are not yet dry through the night. This is really a developmental issue rather than a true behavior problem. Bedwetting occurs because the child's body is not yet mature enough to handle the urine flow at night. This situation is more common in boys than in girls. It also tends to run in families. If both parents were bedwetters, there's a good chance that their child will be, too.

The most important thing to remember is that the child is not wetting the bed on purpose. This is something beyond his voluntary control. Being angry or punishing him isn't going to solve the problem any faster.

Parents can take comfort in the fact that 10 to 15% of bedwetters stop spontaneously each year without any treatment at all. If the child is still enuretic when he's older, treatments can be prescribed by the pediatrician. In the meantime, parents of three year olds can place an absorbent pad under the sheet and try to be patient.

Masturbation

Masturbation is common among young children. They masturbate as a way of exploring their bodies and giving themselves pleasure. Some children masturbate by touching their genitals with their fingers. Others rub up against a blanket or a stuffed toy.

Masturbation is not damaging or harmful. Children should not be shamed or punished for pursuing their curiosity about their bodies. It is important that children not get the idea that their bodies are bad. Once they believe that their bodies are bad, it is a very short jump to believing that they are bad.

Parents need to set limits about where masturbation can occur. Children should be gently reminded that touching themselves is private, not something to be done in public. They should be guided to their bedroom or another appropriate place.

Toileting Refusal, Stool Withholding, and Encopresis

Several kinds of problems with bowel movements can occur in this age group. Some children refuse to defecate in the toilet but happily comply in their pants or in a diaper. Other children actively hold on to stool and fight the urge to have a bowel movement. If stool withholding persists for a long time, it can lead to encopresis (involuntary passage of stool). As the child withholds, he builds up a large amount of hard stool. The intestine becomes so stretched the child loses the feeling that he has to defecate. Soiling occurs as small amounts of liquid stool leak around the blockage. Encopresis is a complicated problem that must be managed by an experienced physician. The goals of therapy are to clean out the retained stool and promote regular toileting habits.

Parents can take steps to prevent such problems. The first is to delay toilet training until the child shows signs of readiness. (See Key 11.) Toileting is one of those areas in which the child has total control. He cannot be forced to defecate on cue. If he is not ready to learn, the process becomes a battle of wills. He will react by refusing to defecate in the toilet or withholding stool altogether.

The toilet must be a comfortable place. A step stool allows the child to climb up by himself. He also needs someplace to balance his feet and bear down as the bowel movement is being passed.

Hard stool is also a common problem. Hard stool causes pain during defecation. The child reacts by withholding stool to avoid additional pain. A diet high in fiber keeps the stool soft. Dried fruit and bran muffins are child-acceptable sources of fiber.

Breath Holding

Breath holding is a phenomenon that was known even to the physicians of ancient Greece. There are two types. The cyanotic (blue) type is much like an elaborate tantrum. The child is prevented from doing something he wants to do, and he begins to cry, hold his breath, and turn blue. He is unresponsive briefly and then resumes breathing on his own. This kind of spell does not cause any damage. It can be avoided, like any tantrum, if the child's attention is diverted during the buildup phase. If not, it is important that the child be in a place where he can't get hurt.

The pallid type is more like a faint. It seems to occur in the particularly sensitive or fearful child. It starts off with an injury, such as a bump on the head. Following this the child goes limp, falls, and turns pale. He recovers quickly. The parental response should focus on reassuring the child and assessing the initial injury.

Cursing

Why do three year olds so readily acquire less than desirable vocabulary? Three year olds recognize the magic of words. When they see adults blush and stammer when certain words are used, they learn that these words have special power.

Three year olds do not understand the literal meanings of curse words or racial epithets. They cannot define other power words, such as love, hate, or dummy, but they are good enough observers to recognize the situations in which they are used by others. It's a tiny step more to utter the words themselves. If they get a big reaction, the performance is repeated again and again.

Controlling this behavior is simple. Parents must provide positive language role models and ignore inappropriate behavior. This requires adults to clean up their acts. Parents are never as aware of how they sound until they live with a three-year-old mimic.

All the people in the child's environment must agree not to laugh at or otherwise encourage his behavior. Sometimes ignoring is not sufficient and a verbal reminder is in order. Parents can say to a child, "That is a word we don't use because it hurts people's feelings." Agree on some words that can be used at times of great frustration. This phase of testing the boundaries of language is self-limited if handled in a matter-of-fact way.

Oppositional Behavior

The oppositional child is uncooperative, aggressive, and prone to frequent temper tantrums. He does what he wants without regard for others. All three year olds are like this from time to time. The child who is this way all the time has a true behavior problem.

Sometimes the kind of discipline used at home is the source of the problem. Children react by being oppositional if discipline is too harsh, inconsistent, or not applied at all.

Dealing with this problem involves teaching parents new ways of interacting with their children. Parents must be able to communicate clear rules, provide positive attention for desired behavior, ignore minor infractions, and know how to use a technique like time-out for misbehavior. (See Key 15 for a more in-depth discussion of discipline.) Parents who recognize oppositional behavior in their child also find the pediatrician to be a good resource and ally.

Behavior problems can be managed successfully. Discuss them with the child's pediatrician, and continue to enjoy the fourth year.

18

SELF-ESTEEM

"Watch me! Look at me! I can climb to the top of the jungle gym. I can swing from the bar. I'm holding on with one hand. Now I'm going to let go."

Carly landed safely in the sand pit. Her parents applauded wildly. She acknowledged their response with a deep bow.

C arly is a child with a high level of self-esteem. She believes in herself. High self-esteem is a precious asset to a child. It is the strength she needs to deal with the challenges of growing up.

How did Carly get this way? How can other families help their children develop this attribute? Answers are provided in this key.

A Positive Cycle

High self-esteem results from experiences with success. When a child does something well, she feels good about herself. When she has many successful experiences, she develops an unshakable belief in her abilities. This belief enriches everything she does. She approaches new tasks eagerly and welcomes challenges. She is confident that she will be successful in the future because she has been successful in the past.

Contributions from the Child

The most natural way to build self-esteem is to identify and build on core abilities in the child. Every child is good at something. It is just a matter of identifying what this is.

Parents can start by asking themselves some questions: What does the child like to do? What kinds of things does she learn easily?

Observing the child also provides answers. Watch what she does during unstructured time. What activities does she select on her own? Her choices are likely to be things that she does well.

Contributions from the Parents

Parents must orchestrate life so that their children encounter success. One way to do this is to support childrens' enthusiasms. Carly's parents, for instance, did this by taking her to the park frequently. This is a place where Carly was able to shine.

Sometimes supporting a child means that parents must rethink their notion of what is appropriate play for boys or girls. A boy may want to dance, and a girl may want to study karate. It is important for parents to be understanding. A three year old's interests may be short-lived, but the feeling of being accepted by his parents will last a lifetime.

There are other ways to guarantee success. Assign the child a simple chore. A three year old can, for instance, set the napkins out on the dinner table. She enjoys success each time she accomplishes this task. A child also enjoys success when she sees her mother go off to work wearing the macaroni necklace she made. Success is seeing her artwork hung on the wall or taped to the refrigerator.

A child can even gain success while mastering a new skill. Success in this situation is defined as a willingness to accept a new challenge, not as achieving perfection on the first try.

The key is to break the task down into a series of small steps. Talk the child through each step. Praise her as she goes along. Realize that it will take longer when she does it on her own, but doing everything for her sends a message that she is not competent. The time spent helping a child master new skills is an investment in her self-worth.

Spending time with a child makes her feel valued. Even 15 minutes spent on an activity of the child's choosing can be meaningful. A child feels special when adults put aside their important grown-up jobs and focus on her. Listen respectfully to her ideas. Ask for her suggestion about which vegetable to make for dinner or which earrings to wear to a party. Being taken seriously by an adult is a wonderful experience for a young child.

Family traditions can also make a child feel special. Mrs. Carmody always made it a practice to take her son, Paul, on her Saturday morning grocery runs. This became such an in-grained aspect of family life that Paul truly thought his mother could not buy groceries without him.

Praise is the currency of self-esteem. Praise can recall a moment of triumph. ("Carly, you were so graceful when you were hanging from the bar with one hand.") Praise can reinforce appropriate behavior. ("Carly, it was so helpful when you put the napkins on the table.")

Praise is most constructive when it is specific. A statement like "It was great when you stopped your tricycle at the corner" is much better than "You are a good girl." The first statement articulates the desired behavior. The child understands what is expected and may be able to do it again. With the second statement, the child may be pleased to be called good but has no idea of the context of the compliment.

Parents also need to be careful about praise by comparison. A compliment like "You are so much more generous than your brother" has an empty ring to it. The child is entitled to know what she did well in her own right ("You were so generous to share your cookies!") rather than triumph at someone else's expense.

Parents can also help a child recognize her own accomplishments. This keeps her from forever being dependent on external sources of praise. Encourage the child to reflect on her own abilities. What does she do well? What does she like to do? When she brings home a painting from school, ask her to point out her favorite part. When she builds a structure with blocks, ask her how she put it together. She is a world authority on herself. Allow her the opportunity to enlighten others.

Barriers to Self-esteem

In addition to personal self-esteem, people develop feelings of worth as a result of their membership in different groups. People take pride as a city when their team wins the World Series. People are elated when a member of their racial or ethnic group wins a Nobel Prize or is elected to the U.S. Senate.

All children can be inspired by high achievers, but nowhere is the need for role models so critical as it is for children who are different. The difference may be membership in a minority group or having a disability. Children who are different need to see people like themselves functioning successfully in the world. These role models are proof that someone who is different can make it. Without the tangible evidence that these role models provide, even the assurances offered by loving and supportive families seem hollow. Self-esteem withers and is replaced by feelings of inferiority and self-hate.

High self-esteem is a priceless gift that parents can give to a child. It can be afforded by any family with an interest in nurturing a child.

19

RELATIONSHIPS

The three year old enjoys a growing network of social relationships. People outside the immediate family circle have an increasingly influential role in the child's life. These people include grandparents, teachers, peers, and even imaginary friends.

Grandparents

Grandparents enrich a child's life in many ways. Their most important contribution is providing unconditional love. They no longer have the prime responsibility for enforcing rules, so they can afford to be a bit more flexible. They may postpone bedtime or allow ice cream before dinner.

Grandparents are also the keepers of the family lore. They are a living link to the family's culture and history. They can contribute to the child's sense of identity. Grandparents are known for their special rituals. One may tell wonderful stories, and another provides drawers full of fascinating objects to explore. Grandparents keep families together by hosting holiday parties and family reunions.

Grandparents provide essential support to parents. Someone who can listen sympathetically, supply advice when asked, and provide occasional babysitting and emergency child care is invaluable. This is an opportunity for adult children and their parents to renew and renegotiate their relationship. Both groups now know what it is like to sit up all night with a sick child or be the target of a temper tantrum. They also both know the joy of nurturing a child and watching her grow.

Successful grandparents are tactful. They recognize that their children are now the ones in charge. They realize that parents want to follow their own inclinations even if this means departing from time-honored practices of the past. They reserve their criticisms in an effort not to undermine parental authority and confidence. When disagreements arise, they are resolved in private among the adults rather than in front of the children. Such issues as giving the children expensive gifts are raised with the parents first before promises are made.

Grandparents who live at a distance can still be important in the life of the child. They can communicate via letter, telephone, or videotape. Visits to each others' homes or family trips can enrich the relationship.

Teachers

Teachers are often the first outside-the-family authority figures three year olds encounter. The relationship is usually very positive. Nursery school teachers are sensitive and patient and seem to know everything. It is no wonder that three year olds regard them with awe and admiration.

In the school environment, three year olds generally behave more conservatively than at home. They are less comfortable and therefore less likely to test the limits. Even so, a teacher still has occasion to admonish inappropriate behavior. This can spark a crisis in her relationship with a child who is used to always getting her way at home. The child is shocked at being reprimanded. The teacher is shocked that the student has not been exposed to discipline at home. Relationships with school staff get off to a better start if limit setting is handled at home.

Parent-teacher communication is essential to meaningful relationships. Teachers need to know about critical events in the lives of their young students. Three year olds do not leave family problems at the doorstep to the classroom. Teachers can respond more effectively to children's needs if they know, for instance, that a parent is ill or there is a new baby on the way.

Peers

Three year olds are ready for real relationships with peers. They can share and take turns. These skills allow them to play with, rather than alongside, other children. Verbal abilities give interactions a chance to flourish and conflicts a chance to resolve.

Children at this age tend to pick friends who are of similar temperament. Two quiet children feel comfortable together. Shared interests are much more important than whether the friend is a boy or a girl. Children tend to have one or two good friends at a time. Friendships may endure or change frequently.

Imaginary Friends

Imaginary friends are a perfectly normal phenomenon at age three. They are the product of an active imagination, not a sign of loneliness or emotional problems.

About 20% of children have imaginary friends. They are most common among first-born children and among girls. The imaginary friend may last as long as six months or may change every day. Sometimes the friend is an animal rather than a person.

Children are usually receptive to adults' questions about their imaginary friends. They enjoy the adults' interest. Although children take their imaginary friends seriously, they are aware that the friends are not real. Parents do not need to remind them of this. The natural course is that children lose interest and give up their imaginary friends on their own.

Parents may want to record some of the characteristics of the friend in the child's scrapbook. This is a wonderful way to remember the vivid imagination of the three year old.

Divorce

Not all relationships are successful. When a marital relationship does not work out, the child learns about divorce.

A three year old has a limited understanding of the world. He sees himself as the center of the universe. Everything that happens somehow relates to him. Thus, when his parents are divorced he feels responsible. He may think that the divorce occurred because he was bad or because his parents no longer love him. He fears that his parents will leave him as they left each other. He strongly wishes for a reconciliation. He may react by developing babyish behavior or sleep problems.

The most important thing that the parents can do is reassure the child that he is still loved. They need to emphasize that their differences were with each other, not with him. Care must be taken to be responsive to the child's needs even as the parents cope with their own emotions. Patience is necessary to deal with the babyish behavior. Change in the child's routine should be kept to a minimum.

Siblings and the extended family are critically important at the time of a divorce. Their continued presence is a welcome reminder to the child that he is not being abandoned and that people care about him.

Long-term issues center on how both parents can maintain an active involvement in the child's life. The nonresident parent should maintain a reliable schedule of visits. If the child travels between two households, it is important that the rules and routines in both places be consistent. It is confusing for a young child to have a set bedtime in one home and then be allowed to go to sleep whenever he pleases in the other.

A child benefits from interacting with people of both sexes. If a child has only sporadic contact with his nonresident father, for instance, another adult male should be designated to serve as a role model.

Divorce is hard on young children. Love, support, and sensitivity can keep it from compromising their development. A wide circle of involved adults helps children meet the challenges of growing up.

20

SIBLINGS

"The baby's really staying here?" asked an incredulous Jordan after seeing his baby brother for the first time.

A new sibling in the family can be a stress even for the most loving and well-prepared three year old. This key presents some ideas that can smooth the transition from single child to sibling.

The Stress of Change

The addition of a new baby means changes in the life of the older child. There are many uncertainties. Who will take him to school in the mornings? Who will read to him at night? Will his parents still love him? Why do they need another baby?

The child's position within the family is altered. He loses his status as the only child or the baby. Things that used to be his are being made ready for someone else.

Sharing the News

The three year old needs to know about the impending birth in advance. It is important not to tell him too early. A three year old does not have a well-developed sense of time. Nine months seems like an eternity. A good time to begin discussions is during the second trimester, when changes in the mother's body become apparent. Try to link the due date to a concrete time that the child knows. ("The baby will be here in the summertime.")

The child's initial reaction may be low-key. Questions begin to emerge as he ponders the information. The questions are usually very basic and center on how a baby will affect his life. Where will the baby sleep? Will it be a brother? Will he play ball with me?

Parents should answer each question simply and directly as it comes up rather than deliver an exhaustive lecture that tries to anticipate all of the child's concerns. He will be sure to ask follow-up questions if he is not satisfied. It is important to emphasize that the sibling will be an infant, not a peer. There is nothing more disappointing for a child who has envisioned a playmate than the reality of a crying, sleeping, eating, not even able to sit up newborn.

Sharing the Preparation

A three year old may enjoy becoming involved in the preparations for the baby's arrival. He can help arrange the baby's room or accompany his mother to her prenatal visits and hear the fetal heartbeat. These activities are meaningful only if the child is really interested. There is no benefit to insisting that he participate. This only makes him resentful.

Preparation often involves refurbishing the older child's crib, stroller, or high chair for the baby's use. Some children dislike the idea of another child inheriting their things. Strong feelings can be evoked even if they haven't used these items in years. It is, of course, the symbolism of these events, not the actual handing down, that is bothersome. He is being asked to share his crib, his stroller, his high chair, his car seat, his room, and his parents. Where does it end? He feels pushed aside and diminished in importance.

Parents can soften the blow by reminding the child that he really doesn't need these things anymore. Look through the child's baby toys together, and let him choose one or two that he doesn't want to share with the new baby. Put them away in a special place so that the child knows that those toys will always be his. If the child is going to be moved out of the crib so the baby can use it, do this several months in advance to ensure that he does not feel pushed out.

This is also a good time to get out the child's baby scrapbook. He doesn't remember when he was the focus of this special kind of attention. Seeing the pictures reassures him that he received his quota of intense nurturing.

Time during the pregnancy should also be spent cementing the child's relationships with family members other than his mother. If Grandma is familiar with his bedtime routine and Dad knows how to cut his sandwiches just the right way, then Mom can get some additional rest. These supports will be even more critical once the baby actually arrives.

Parents sometimes develop an accelerated agenda for the child during the pregnancy. They would like him all grown up: out of diapers, sleeping through the night in a real bed, and established in nursery school before the baby comes. It is not realistic to expect so many fundamental changes to occur within a short period of time. Developmental progress occurs most readily on the child's own timetable. Rather than pressure him, use the time during the pregnancy to savor the relationship with the older child.

Many hospitals offer a sibling class to prepare older children for a baby's birth. The class involves doll play and a tour of the nursery. It may also be helpful to the child to learn that he is not the only one going through this rite of passage.

Birth and Homecoming
Separation from the mother when she goes to the hospital for delivery is a particularly stressful time for the three year

old. Let him know in advance about the arrangements that have been made for his care. He will want to know where he will be staying and who will be taking care of him. If he will be able to visit his mother on the maternity ward, be sure to specify this.

Advance planning can make the separation more bearable. The mother can tape some songs or stories that can be played for the child while she is in the hospital. She can also hide some notes or small gifts around the house for the child to discover while she's away. Telephone contact is important, particularly if the child will not be allowed to visit.

The child's initial reaction to his sibling can range from detestation to delight. The child may even seem indifferent. A child who acts as if he doesn't care is often feeling hurt, abandoned, and left out. In this situation, parents should make special mention of how much they missed him while they were at the hospital. He will be greatly relieved by their display, even if he doesn't show it.

Some parents bring home a special toy and tell the older child it is a gift from the baby. More important than any toy, however, is attention. The child needs lots of physical affection to balance what he sees the newborn receiving. He also needs to have some one-on-one time with his mother to reassure him that their relationship is still important and vital.

Some children act more babyish after the newborn arrives. Recent developmental acquisitions vanish. He begs to breast-feed and demands to use diapers. This regression is normal and quite logical from the child's point of view. He sees the baby getting a lot of attention. He figures that if he acts more helpless people will pay more attention to him.

The best response is to find a way to give him the attention he wants while supporting age-appropriate activities. Instead of breast-feeding, let him sit on his mother's lap while he drinks a cup of juice. If he still insists on using diapers or drinking from a bottle, this is not worth a major battle. He will soon find that acting like a baby does not make him feel particularly good, and he will give up these behaviors on his own.

Help the child develop pride in his new role as the older sibling. Remark on how the baby smiles particularly broadly when he is around. When the baby coos or cries, ask the older child to interpret what his sibling is saying. Allow the older child to touch or hold the baby under supervision. Excluding him from these activities sends a message of mistrust that can really intensify resentment.

Older Siblings

Older siblings are useful. They have broken in the inexperienced parents and absorbed their rookie miscues. Older siblings serve as mentors and role models. They are pals, coconspirators, and confidantes. Older siblings provide a window into a world that includes school, birthday parties, and sleepovers. The advantage for a younger child is a richer and less sheltered life. The complaint is that he never gets to do anything first.

The challenge for parents is to treat the children fairly. Equal treatment is an impossible standard when dealing with different personalities at different stages of development. If parents can balance the children's needs, this should be sufficient. Siblings are natural allies. There are more things that unite them than divide them. If they have time together without parental interference, the relationship will flourish.

The sibling relationship is an important facet of family life. It is a positive reflection on parents when siblings end up as friends.

21

DIFFICULT SUBJECTS: TALKING ABOUT BIRTH AND DEATH

C hildren ask difficult questions. They ask them in loud voices, frequently in public places. Parents must be prepared to deal with both the informational and emotional implications of their childrens' questions. This key can help them get ready.

Childrens' questions must be answered directly, simply, and honestly. Three year olds sense when they're being brushed off or not taken seriously. They wonder if they've done something wrong by asking. If parents want their children to continue to come to them with questions, they must set a precedent of supplying answers.

A simple answer is sufficient. Children don't have the patience or cognitive ability to process complicated explanations. Too much information can be overwhelming. Be assured that they will come back with further questions if they are not satisfied. Often they want to hear the same explanation over and over. Their questions frequently elicit unbelievable information. They need to make sure that they've gotten it right.

Parents can check the child's understanding by asking him to repeat the explanation back. Sometimes the child is confused by new vocabulary or concepts. This process gives parents an immediate opportunity to clarify misconceptions.

Honesty is crucial. The information given should be accurate. It is awkward to give an explanation one year and then totally revamp it the next. This kind of treatment erodes a child's trust. A child will not confide in someone he doesn't trust.

Talking About Birth

"How do you get adults?" asked Dylan. His mother took a deep breath and launched into a lengthy explanation about eggs growing inside a mother's body. "No, no, no," said Dylan, clearly exasperated, "Are you born an adult or do you grow one?"

Children are curious about their origins. They usually start by learning that the baby grows inside the mother. The next, very practical, consideration is how the baby gets out. Most parents are comfortable with the explanation that the baby emerges through a special opening that can stretch very wide.

The next question concerns how babies get started. Parents offer various explanations for this one depending on their personal beliefs. Some talk about planting a seed, others talk about exchanging love, and still others talk about gifts from God.

Three year olds process this information on a very personal level. Both boys and girls worry about suddenly finding themselves pregnant. It is important to tell them that people must be grown up to have babies. They should know that only women have the special place where babies can grow. They

103

will be reassured to learn that pregnancy is not a spontaneous event but the culmination of a process.

A discussion of origins can prompt a particularly perceptive child to realize that there was a time when he did not exist. This is a staggering revelation! The shock can be blunted by reassuring him about how special life has been since his arrival. This discussion can be reinforced by looking over his baby album and the many memorable events it documents.

Adoption

Questions about birth can be particularly sensitive for adoptive parents. Three is a good age at which to introduce the subject of adoption. A three year old can understand that he grew inside the body of a woman other than his adoptive mother. Explaining the reasons behind the adoption is a delicate matter because the child can so easily feel rejected by the birth parents. Many families explain that the birth parents were unable to take care of him and arranged for him to have a loving home. He needs to be reassured that the adoption is permanent and that his adoptive parents will always be there to take care of him.

Some parents, in an effort to make the child feel special, tell him that he was selected for their family over all other children. Young children process this well-meaning explanation in a concrete way. They envision a vast department store with rows and rows of children. The explanation can backfire because it raises the specter of impermanence. Children have witnessed items being returned to the store and worry that they, too, might be returned if they do something wrong.

Parents will return to the subject of adoption many times as the child grows. He will have more questions about his birth parents and the adoption process. This is normal curiosity and should not be interpreted as hostility or ingratitude.

Talking About Death

Diana: "I live with my parents."

Her mother: "That's right."

Diana: "Do you live with your parents?"

Her mother: "No. Your grandma is my mother. We don't live with her."

Diana: "Does Grandma live with her parents?"

Her mother: "No. Her mother is your great-grandmother."

Diana: "Does Great-grandma live with her parents?"

Her mother: "No. Her parents aren't alive any more."

Diana: "They died."

Her mother: "Yes, that's right. They were very old. They lived a long time."

Diana: "Did she say good-bye to them?"

Her mother: "Yes, I'm sure she did."

Diana: "Did she say she loved them?"

Her mother: "Yes."

Diana: "And they still died? Are you going to die?"

Her mother: "I'm very healthy and I take good care of myself. I don't expect to die until I'm very old."

Diana: "Don't get old. If you die, I won't have a mother. I love you. I don't want you to die."

Children learn about death in different ways. Some learn firsthand from the death of a plant, a pet, or a person. Others, like Diana, discover the concept before they have any personal experience with it.

Childrens' reactions are personal and immediate. Will I die if I get sick? Who will take care of me if my parents die? As Diana put it, "If you die, I won't have a mother."

Children don't understand that death is permanent. They experience death as a separation. They expect, as has been their experience with other separations, that the person will return eventually.

Death defies many of the fundamental beliefs children have about how the world works. Three year olds believe that their thoughts have power over external events. In her conversation with her mother, Diana received some startling information. She found out that even love, the strongest emotion she knows, is powerless to prevent death.

Three year olds have difficulty understanding how the person died. This difficulty stems from their immature notions of cause and effect. They have trouble figuring out how one thing can cause another thing to occur. They can't envision how an illness or an accident could result in death. They may feel it was something they did or said that caused the death to occur.

Concrete thinking demands exact answers to unanswerable questions. Children want to know heaven's exact location. They want to know why someone they loved had to die. Concrete thinking is also responsible for solutions of elegant simplicity, however. As Diana suggested, "Don't get old."

Helping a Child Deal with Death

There are a number of things that adults can do to help a child deal with death. The first is to emphasize that death is a permanent state. Remind the child about plants or flowers that died and didn't come back. Be careful about the specific words that are used. Phrases like "went away" and "at rest" can cause confusion. As one child said, "Hasn't Grandpa rested enough?"

Children have a difficult time accepting that death happens without a reason. Question them about why they think the person died. This is an opportunity to straighten out misconceptions and provide reassurance that no one was at fault.

Talk with the child about her memories of the person. Help her remember what they liked about each other and what they liked to do together. The child might like a photograph of the person or an object that belonged to him.

Reassure the child that a dead person has no feelings or physical needs. Children become very worried that the dead person will be cold, hungry, or lonely.

The issue of whether the child should attend the funeral is difficult. She may find comfort in the rituals or be distressed at the sight of so many grief-stricken adults. If the child is to attend, she should be prepared in advance so she knows exactly what to expect. A close friend or family member should be assigned to stay with her. If she becomes overwhelmed, she and her companion can leave.

Children express their grief in various ways. They may seem tired, clingy, nervous, or overly active rather than sad. They may engage in destructive behavior or develop problems sleeping. They may play make-believe funeral.

All these reactions are normal and expectable. Play, in particular, is a very healthy way of coping with the new sights, sounds, and feelings. Extra patience and reassurance from trusted adults can help a child survive this traumatic time.

Direct, simple, and honest responses to childrens' questions will provide them with the information they need.

22

RAISING A BRIGHT CHILD

A All parents want their children to be bright. Early learning experiences at home can give children the background they need to succeed in school and in life. This key highlights what parents can do to stimulate their children's thinking.

At three, it is too early for quantum physics, but it is exactly the right time to stimulate a love of learning, encourage curiosity, and build self-esteem. Appropriate play activities develop these attributes. With these attributes in place, the child is ready to tackle physics or any other subject that interests her at the appropriate time.

Bright children need more than facts. They need to know how to use information. They need to know how to make judgments, interpret what they see, and apply what they've learned in the past to new situations. They must be able to see different sides of a problem. Truly creative thinking means generating multiple solutions to a problem rather than merely a single reflexive response.

Stimulating Language Skills

A child's love of learning is set in motion by her early experiences with books. Her first reading lesson takes place long before the first grade. It takes place on her parent's lap as she snuggles up close to hear a story read. She becomes captivated by the sounds and rhythms of the words and the beauty and color of the illustrations. This wonderful experience fosters a love of books and the desire to become a good reader.

Through reading, a child is introduced to writing. She realizes that the black squiggles on the page are a kind of code. It is this special code that confers a permanent life to the story.

Even a young child can participate in the writing process. She can dictate a caption to one of her paintings. She can compose a thank-you note or add to a grocery list. She can scribble her own letter and then "read" it back. When someone writes down what she said, she feels important. This also allows her to have the magical experience of going back to her own words.

Verbal communication is also a key form of expression. When a child talks, she is learning to organize her thoughts, present them in a logical sequence, utilize vocabulary, and practice grammatical structures. Listen to what the child has to say. It adds to a child's confidence when the adults around her pay serious attention to her thoughts and feelings. Set up a supportive atmosphere in which the child feels comfortable thinking out loud. If she knows she won't be ridiculed or corrected, she is more likely to take intellectual chances. Original thinking is the hallmark of the creative and successful student.

The dinner table is a great place for family conversation. The child can contribute by talking about what she did during the day, reciting a nursery rhyme, or asking a riddle.

Stimulating Math Skills

Advanced math skills build on the ability to sort and categorize objects. Young children are ready to learn the concepts of same and different. These skills can be practiced even while doing the laundry. Laundry can be sorted along a number of dimensions. Items can be divided by owner or by color. The child is learning while a necessary chore is being done.

A three year old can also learn to sort according to shape. A shape classification game can be prepared by cutting various shapes from pieces of construction paper of different colors. Spread them out on the floor, and have the child gather up those that are the same. After she can do this with shapes, try it with alphabet letters. A more difficult variation is to sort according to two dimensions by picking up only the red triangles or the purple circles.

Measuring gives the child hands-on experience with the concepts of more, less, long, and short. A set of measuring cups in the bathtub is a great deal of fun. Things that grow are also ideal objects to measure. Plant some fast-growing seeds with the child, and measure them daily. Parents can even demonstrate how to keep a record of the plant's growth.

A three year old is ready for some basic number concepts. She can learn to count by rote. Once she can do this, she will energetically count the objects she encounters in her world: steps on the staircase, cars on the street, people on line at the bank. She also comes to understand that the number 1 corresponds to a single object. She learns that larger numbers mean more objects and smaller numbers mean fewer. A good way to illustrate this is with playing cards because they feature both the number symbol and the requisite number of hearts or clubs on the faces.

Stimulating Observational Skills

Children need good observational skills. Looking at shapes is an excellent way to enhance them. Shapes are everywhere. Challenge the child to point out circles, squares, and triangles in household items. This game can also be played outdoors. Once the child thoroughly understands shapes, challenge her to compare them in terms of size.

Puzzles also develop a child's observational and problem-solving skills. She must figure out how the individual shapes relate to one another to form an overall pattern. Puzzle working is an exercise in patience and tenacity as well.

Observation is not only visual. A child's tactile sense can be developed using a feeling box. Place objects of different textures (a smooth stone, a piece of sandpaper, or a scrap of velvet cloth) into a shoe box or large paper bag. Have the child close her eyes, reach into the bag, and select an object. With her eyes still closed, ask her to describe the object and guess what it is.

Challenge her auditory sense by having her identify common sounds in her environment, such as a doorbell, car horn, or vacuum cleaner. Clap out a simple rhythm, and have her imitate it.

Play a tasting game by feeding her a tiny bit of food while she has her eyes closed. See if she can identify a banana, a pickle, or a chocolate chip by its taste.

Stimulating Thinking

Children need practice in putting information together, drawing conclusions, and making predictions. This is the basis of scientific thinking. Doing science with young children does not mean stocking the house with dangerous chemicals and test tubes. It means asking the question, "What do you think will happen?" and then finding out. This is a very natural process to young children, who depend heavily on seeing, touching, and doing to learn. Experiments that charm three year olds are as simple as adding food coloring to water or leaving a dish of water outside in the hot sun. Children who love water play also enjoy collecting objects and then trying to guess which will sink and which ones will float.

A good memory is also a valuable asset. Challenge the child to name as many animals or colors as she can. A simplified version of the party game, Concentration, is fun for a three year old. Line up three distinct but familiar objects. Ask the child to study them and then close her eyes. Remove one object. Then ask the child to open her eyes and guess which is missing. When she masters this, add more objects or remove two at a time.

The Role of Television

Television can be a learning tool. It is also a boon to parents when it provides safe, convenient, and no-fuss entertainment for children.

Television viewing must be regulated and supervised. It is a passive experience that cuts into the time when children could be actively engaged in creative play. Excessive television viewing has been linked to obesity and decreased attention spans in children. Violent shows can make children aggressive, fearful, and prone to nightmares.

Television viewing must be balanced with other priorities in the child's life so that it does not pose a threat to learning.

The Stressed Child

Sometimes parents place too much emphasis on early learning. The result is the stressed child syndrome.

"Marisol can recite the names of all of the presidents of the United States in chronological order," boasted Mr. Gomez. "Go ahead, Marisol."
"Washington, Adams, Jefferson," she began haltingly. She was completely stuck after Monroe.
"What is a president, anyway, Marisol?" asked one of the spectators.
"I don't know," she responded.

Marisol is a typical stressed child. She is being pushed to handle information and activities that are beyond the capacities of a child her age.

A stressed child starts with stressed parents. Stressed parents are intensely concerned about how their child will fare in the future. They are obsessed with how she compares to her peers. Their competitive natures focus on the child's education. They want her to be first: first to read, first to write, and first to master a musical instrument.

Pushy parents live through their children's accomplishments. Marisol's subject was the presidency not because she showed any interest in the area but simply because her father was a history buff.

Stressed children pay a heavy price. They live under an intense pressure to achieve and perform. Marisol was used to being trotted out at her parents' parties to recite the list. Stressed children feel that parental love is contingent on their accomplishments. Marisol felt a responsibility to make her parents happy. She knew they were happy when she got through the list. She felt their keen disappointment when she did not.

Young children do not need this kind of pressure to learn. They learn easily when their interests are supported and nurtured. Education is not a race. The child who learns to read at three is not necessarily a better adult reader than the one who learns at seven. The best head start for learning is a secure, stimulating, and responsive familial environment.

There are many opportunities to teach embedded in the activities of daily life. Discovering them benefits both the child and the parents.

23

RAISING A READER

All parents want their children to be excellent and enthusiastic readers. Parents recognize that reading is the key to personal growth and academic success. Positive associations with reading start in childhood. If a child enjoys being read to, he is motivated to learn to read by himself. This key explores the many benefits of reading and suggests ways that families can enjoy the magic of words.

Benefits of Reading

Reading involves new adventures. Through books, a child can visit the moon or travel back in time to the age of the dinosaurs. These experiences challenge the child's understanding of the world and help to develop his imagination.

Children also enjoy stories that involve familiar events. Many of these stories feature animals as the main characters. Children empathize as Curious George visits the dentist, Francis the raccoon copes with a baby sister, or Corduroy finds a friend.

These stories present children with positive models for coping. They get ideas about how to handle similar situations in their own lives. They also learn that they are not alone in having to face difficult situations.

There are intellectual benefits to reading. New vocabulary and concepts can be introduced through books. Parents can point out various colors or animals that are depicted in the illustrations. Letters and numbers can be taught using various alphabet and counting books. It is preferable to concentrate on one or two things at a time rather than overwhelm the child with a lot of new information.

Through reading, children make the association between the spoken and the written word. They realize that the black squiggles on the page represent the story. They recognize the importance of writing in making the story accessible to people. They are motivated to become one of those people who can turn marks on a page into fascinating adventures.

Reading also develops a child's listening and thinking skills. The child's attention span lengthens as he stays focused to hear how the story turns out. He becomes actively involved if the parent asks him which character he likes or what he imagines will happen next.

Reading also stretches a child's memory. A three year old may be able to recite his favorite book by heart. If a parent substitutes a word or tries to skip a page, expect a major commotion. A child this age loves to catch adults making mistakes.

Reading is a time for physical closeness. It is fun to snuggle in a chair or huddle together under blankets and read a story. The positive feelings generated by this situation generalize to the books themselves. A lifelong love of learning begins.

Children quickly recognize the importance adults place on books. Their read-to-me requests are sometimes thinly veiled pleas for attention or a cuddle. This is one situation in which a parent can give in and still feel good.

Tips from Professional Storytellers

Read at a relaxed pace. Even if there are dishes to wash, deadlines to meet, or lunches to prepare, take time to enjoy this special activity. A special mood can't be established in a tense and rushed atmosphere.

Check out the book before reading it to the child. Make sure that the vocabulary is age appropriate. See whether the length of the story matches the child's attention span. Look carefully at the content. Is the message suitable? Is the story too scary? Does it promote racial or ethnic stereotypes?

Readers are not locked into the text. An alphabet book does not have to be used only to teach about letters. The lovely illustrations can serve as great vocabulary builders. Sometimes just looking at the pictures and pointing out different objects can be fun. Text that is too lengthy or complicated can be paraphrased or summarized. Sometimes a child's interest wanes if too much time is spent on a particular page. If the child seems bored, move on or take a break. A book need not be read cover to cover at a single sitting.

Use an expressive voice to read. Try using different vocal characteristics for each of the characters in the story.

Let the child choose the book from among those that the parent has reviewed. This is one area in which he can safely exercise his autonomy. Although it can be humbling, try to respect the child's preferences. One parent scoured the library system for a copy of an out-of-print treasure she remembered from her childhood. When she triumphantly presented the book to her daughter, she was informed that the story was "dumb."

Remember that children love repetition. It's normal for them to ask for the same book to be read over and over. There's a sense of security in finding that the words are always the same. It is reassuring when the characters end up living happily ever after every time.

Make time for reading every day. Reading time is an investment in a child's learning ability. Even 15 minutes a day is a good start. When fatigue makes the letters on the page an absolute blur, pick a familiar book and let the child tell the story.

Adults should model reading behavior for the child. Make sure that she sees the important adults in her life reading books, magazines, or newspapers on a daily basis. Adults who have difficulty reading or want to improve their skills should contact local schools or community agencies regarding literacy classes.

Good Book Choices

Children enjoy books with a gimmick. Texts written in rhyme are great for three year olds. They love to chime in with the right word at the end of the line. Books that contain a repeating phrase or pattern draw children into the story. Pop-up books, musical books, and glow in the dark books are also fun.

Wordless books are versatile. They can be short stories for an impatient child or a springboard for the imagination of a highly verbal child. A full listing of recommended books for three year olds is contained in Books for Children.

Reading with a child is a magical experience. It is an introduction to fascinating people and wonderful places. Positive feelings about reading start early and stay with a child for a lifetime.

24

RAISING A CREATIVE CHILD

A rt activities provide stimulating learning experiences for young children. Three year olds learn best by touching, manipulating, and actively exploring their world. These inclinations make three year olds natural artists.

Art as Learning

Artwork is a way for children to express ideas and communicate with others. Some children find it much easier to use paint than to use words.

Art teaches children about the use of symbols. Children draw circles and lines to represent objects. This is the foundation for learning how to write. In time, the circles and lines are used to form letters, words, and sentences.

Art teaches children about the use of space. As they organize shapes on a page, they learn about the orderly use of space. This is important because, to read, children must understand how text is arranged on a page from top to bottom and from left to right.

Artwork is a way for a child to create something unique. No one else could have created that painting in precisely the same way. She makes decisions. She chooses the shapes to draw, the colors to use, and the placement of the objects on the page.

Art and Development

A child's first art experience is scribbling. By two, she explores the relationship between various arm and hand movements and the shapes they produce on the page. She learns about the consequences of straying outside the boundaries of her paper. The excitement is not in the finished product but in having an effect on the environment.

A three year old has better motor control. She can produce a discrete circle because she can limit her arm movement to a single rotation. Better motor control also means she can choose to place that circle in a specific spot on the paper. The lines, themselves, are firmer thanks to a more secure pencil grip.

Circles can then be repeated, joined with lines, and speckled with dots to form more complex abstract designs. Between the ages of three and four, the child suddenly realizes that the collection of scribbles reminds her of something. "That looks like a zebra," she thinks. At this age the child labels the drawing after she has finished it. It is not until after the age of five that a child sits down with a blank piece of paper and decides what to draw in advance.

Painting

The progression in painting is different, reflecting the challenges of a more fluid medium. At first, the three year old applies separate tentative strokes to the paper. She then moves on to painting big patches of color. Experimentation with overlapping colors usually results in a big brown painting. With practice, the child learns to apply colors side by side without intermixing. She eventually learns to use the brush more like a writing tool and develops the skill to outline in one color and fill in with another.

Human Figure Drawings

A three year old can draw a primitive human face. It has a circle for a head, eyes, and perhaps a mouth. By four, the human figure has spokes radiating from the circle representing arms and legs. This classic form is called the sun figure.

Getting Started

Parents greatly influence their childrens' feelings about art. Active encouragement helps children move more quickly and confidently through the stages of artistic expression.

Parents can help in a practical way by providing art materials and a work space. The work space should be an area in which the child need not worry about making a mess. It can be a kitchen table, floor space covered by newspapers, a low table, or even a plywood board balanced on cinder blocks. A fancy easel is actually less optimal because paint drips more readily on an angled surface.

Crayons have great appeal for young artists. Large crayons are well suited for small hands. Some crayons are made flat on one side so that they do not roll away. Small children may not be able to exert a lot of pressure on a crayon, so choose one that makes a vivid mark even when handled lightly. Parents should look for crayons that are washable and nontoxic.

Sometimes a pristine box of crayons intimidates a child. She doesn't want to use them for fear of ruining them. If this is the case, help her along by peeling down the paper or breaking a few.

Tempera paint is also fun. Provide children with the basic colors—red, yellow, blue, black, and white. Let them discover the joy of mixing colors. Other necessary items for painting include short bristled brushes, nonspill cups to hold the paint and water, and paper. Newsprint, 18×24 inches, is a good size for children who are just learning how to manage space.

Other desirable art materials include nontoxic washable markers, play doughs, tape, glue, scissors, and scraps. Books with craft ideas are listed in Activity Books for Adults.

Supporting the Young Artist

The kind of feedback the child receives influences her feelings about art and her feelings about herself. This is a time to let the child make her own decisions and do things her own way. It hurts no one if she chooses to paint the grass orange and the sky green. The emphasis should be on expressing herself and having fun.

Let the child determine when she is finished rather than sending her back to add more details. She may work longer, however, if an adult is standing by and providing encouragement.

Parents must squelch the temptation to improve upon the child's work. When a parent jumps in to add details or make things look a little more realistic, it sends the child a negative message about her capabilities. The process of making art is far more important than the product.

Parents should be judicious in their comments. "What is this supposed to be?" delivers a crushing blow to a child who has worked really hard on a drawing. "Those are really nice colors you used" is a much more supportive statement which is suitable to almost any occasion. Such responses as "Tell me about this picture" or "How did you do this?" set the child up as an authority figure and send a respectful message about her efforts and achievements.

A display area, such as a bulletin board, demonstrates to the child how much her work is valued. A long hallway can serve as a gallery space. The child's drawings can even be hung amid works by other family members. Dating the pictures provides an ideal way of recalling the child's artistic development.

Art activities are fun and engaging. In addition, they are a wonderful paradigm for learning. The skills practiced while drawing and painting are important building blocks for academic and personal success.

25

RAISING A SPOILED CHILD

*"I want my book," demanded Andre. "Give it back. Give it back **now.**" Andre snatched the book out of the hands of his unsuspecting older brother. He threw it to the ground and stomped on it. Tears were flowing wildly. He reached down to get it, picked it up, and tore off its cover. Then he tore out page after page and ripped each one to shreds. His brother looked on in amazement.*

Andre is a spoiled child. He is demanding, destructive, and easily frustrated. He insists on getting his way in every situation. He has difficulty getting along with others. He is unhappy and makes the people around him unhappy as well.

Spoiled children exhibit self-centered and immature behavior. They show a lack of consideration for others. They fail to follow household rules and may even refuse to eat and sleep. They make unreasonable demands. Yet, even when their demands are met, they are not satisfied for very long. They react to the most trivial amounts of frustration with tantrums, whining, biting, and kicking.

Development of the Spoiled Child

A child becomes a tyrant when his parents fail to set appropriate limits for his behavior. If a child's demands are always met, he comes to expect instant action from everyone. If he gets his way whenever he whines or has a tantrum, he never learns a more appropriate way to act. If he is not taught to share, he grabs whatever toy he wants.

Parents do not set out to spoil a child intentionally. It happens because setting limits is such a difficult and time-consuming task. When confrontations occur, it seems easier at the moment to patch things up quickly and leave the major rule teaching for another time. Because Major Rule Teaching Day never comes, however, maladaptive behavior patterns persist.

Parents who are short of energy, time, or confidence in their caretaking abilities find it especially hard to enforce rules. Working parents are in a particular bind. They already feel guilty about the limited time they spend with their children. They do not want their time together marred by unpleasantness. They end up by giving in to their children's demands.

Another kind of spoiling occurs when there is confusion between a child's needs and a child's whims. At a store, for example, a child may cry bitterly and convince his parents that his survival is entirely based on having a "Shaggy the Dog" puppet. The parents purchase Shaggy to quell the tears. The next day, the parents are horrified to find Shaggy, abandoned and unloved, under the kitchen table. The child is so used to getting things that even expensive toys no longer have any meaning.

Living with a spoiled child is a tremendous stress. Parents feel angry and frustrated. Some are so demoralized that they give up and allow the child to do whatever he wants. Others respond by yelling at or even hitting the child. These tactics do not help and serve only to make the problem worse.

Spoiling affects more than the immediate family. A spoiled child is not popular with his peers. Teachers resent having to deal with a spoiled child in the classroom. They believe that a respect for rules is something that should be taught at home.

Dealing with Spoiled Behavior

The best approach to spoiled behavior is prevention. It is much more effective to introduce rules as they are needed. Children naturally absorb them incrementally, day by day. Their behavior is then shaped by constant exposure to a gentle but pervasive kind of guidance.

Spoiled behavior can be reversed. The strategy is to start with a few simple rules that target intrusive or dangerous behavior. The rules must be clear, nonnegotiable, and consistently enforced. For instance, if the child is not in his car seat, the car does not go forward. Once the child masters the priority rules, others can be added.

Use time-out if the child does not comply with the rules. A full discussion of the time-out technique is contained in Key 15. There is no role for teasing, threatening, punishing, or spanking. The child should learn to follow rules not out of fear but because they reflect appropriate standards.

The demanding child can be helped by two approaches. Both aim to teach him to cope with the experience of not having his needs met immediately. One approach is to encourage the child to be more self-reliant. ("Andre, why don't you try and put the shirt on yourself?") Provide lots of praise for anything that could be construed as an attempt.

A delaying strategy is another option. Let him know that he will be helped, but not immediately. Give him a clear and concrete time frame, and be sure to stick to it. ("Andre, I will be there as soon as I finish writing this paragraph.") Keep expanding the delay time bit by bit until the child can wait comfortably for a few minutes.

The child reacts to the tightening of the rules by testing parental resolve. He may cry or have a tantrum. He may hit or throw things. It is absolutely critical to stand firm. If his parents don't give in no matter how outrageous his behavior, the child realizes that they are really serious about making the changes. Progress can then begin in earnest.

Is He Truly Spoiled?

Some normal situations can be mistaken for spoiled behavior. A curious child who is constantly touching things that don't belong to him is often called spoiled. This type of exploration is normal and necessary for a young child's development. The logical response to this behavior is to child-proof the home and remove all dangerous or fragile objects. Simultaneously, the child must be taught the meaning of the word *no*. He just cannot pick up every interesting-looking object.

The word *spoiled* is also applied to the independent and stubborn child who is just starting to voice his own views. People see his steadfastness and think he's acting spoiled. A young child who is learning to be independent clings ferociously to his ideas because they define who he is. They are his identity. His actions stem from immaturity, not from maliciousness.

A number of developmental problems are frequently confused with spoiled behavior. These include speech and hearing problems, autism, temperamental problems, and attention deficit disorder. A child dealing with a chronic illness or his parents' divorce may be stressed, not spoiled.

Spoiled behavior does not indicate a child who is beyond hope. Loving guidance can improve his behavior and provide a happier outcome for both the parents and the child.

26

~~~~~~

RAISING A SPECIAL CHILD

Raising any child is a challenge. There are some special situations that represent particular challenges. This key highlights three of them.

The Gifted Child

My three-year-old daughter reads.

My three-year-old son plays the violin.

My three-year-old son ice skates.

My three-year-old daughter programs our VCR.

All these parents are expressing the hope that their child is gifted. Having a gift is an advantage. It makes the child special. It is a source of self-esteem. It can be the basis of an enjoyable hobby or a lucrative career. The process of identifying and nurturing young talent is the focus of this section.

Definitions of Giftedness

Giftedness can be defined in several ways. The traditional criterion is an intelligence quotient score of 130 or more. A score in this range places an individual in the top 2% of the population.

This view of giftedness is uncomfortably narrow. A broader definition takes into consideration a child's special talents. A child who sings well or is an exceptional athlete is gifted. Another child's gift may be a deep sensitivity to the feelings of others or an ability to understand the workings of mechanical objects. These children may not excel on standardized tests but clearly have special abilities.

Behavior of Gifted Children

Gifted young children exhibit a number of characteristic behaviors. They tend to have large vocabularies and a history of speaking at an early age. They show precocious interest and ability in academic skills, such as recognizing letters and writing words. They may even teach themselves to read before entering school.

Math skills also emerge early. Gifted young children can count, do simple arithmetic, tell time, and describe the value of different denominations of money.

Curiosity is a key sign of giftedness. Gifted children want to know how things work. They acquire information easily and are able to make creative associations between ideas. They ask wonderful questions: Why do people have to die? Who was the first person on earth? One of their passions is collecting things—rocks, shells, or even golf balls.

Gifted children have excellent memories. They may know the lyrics to dozens of songs or have the ability to identify even obscure types of dinosaurs. They show an amazing ability to concentrate on the things that interest them. They appreciate humor.

Gifted children tend to seek out older playmates who may be more satisfying companions than their peers. It is important to remember that although they are intellectually advanced, their social and emotional development is on par with their chronological age. They need age-appropriate limits and discipline.

How Parents Can Help

Parents can help by providing opportunities for exploration and discovery. Reading, following up on the child's interests, taking neighborhood walks, and talking about these experiences are key activities. Three year olds, even those who are gifted, do not need formal academic training. Gifted children need to be challenged but do not need to be pushed.

The Child with a Chronic Illness

The child with a chronic illness must deal with medical treatments, pain, and frequent hospitalizations in addition to the usual stresses of growing up. This section outlines the special supports families can implement to keep the focus on normal development.

Challenges of Chronic Illness

The first challenge is to provide children with a developmentally appropriate explanation of what is wrong. This is difficult because young children have a limited understanding of illness. They think that illness is a punishment for some bad thought or deed. They believe that it was their fault that they got sick.

Children also have difficulty understanding the treatment aspect. They cannot see how a painful treatment could be beneficial.

A major concern is how the illness affects his daily life. The more restrictions it imposes, the more burdensome it seems. A child who has to have daily medications, treatment, or therapy sees illness as a big part of his life. A hospitalization, which completely disrupts his schedule, is a major upheaval.

Chronic illness complicates development. Three year olds want to do everything for themselves. They are eager to be physically active. Social experiences with other children are a key feature of their world.

Medical considerations may curtail some of these experiences for the chronically ill child. He may not have the endurance for normal playground activities. Interactions with peers may be limited because of frequent hospitalizations or concerns about infection. This leaves a child with a chronic illness at risk for dependency, fearfulness, passivity, and low self-esteem.

How Parents Can Help

Parents can help by keeping the child's life as normal as possible. This means treating the child like other family members. He should be expected to do chores and follow the household rules. He should be subject to disciplinary action when he behaves inappropriately.

Allow the child to participate in age-appropriate activities. Try to avoid overprotecting him. An asthmatic child can run as long as he knows the bodily signals that indicate that he should stop. If the child cannot attend a preschool, arrange for children to come over to the house to play. Look for ways to build up the child's strengths. If his activity must be limited, perhaps block play or painting will become his forte.

Let the child assist in his own care. This enhances his feelings of being independent and in control. He can decide to take his medicine in three gulps rather than four or lay out the equipment needed for a dressing change.

Support the child when he must be hospitalized. Parents play a key role in bridging the gap between home and hospital. Bring along the child's favorite stuffed animal or blanket. Perhaps he can even be allowed to wear his own pajamas or robe. Maintaining interaction with friends is important. Let people know that the child would like to hear from them. A card from a friend or a call from a teacher can really lift morale.

Increasing numbers of children with serious illnesses are surviving to adulthood. Attention to their developmental needs ensures that they are emotionally as well as physically healthy.

The Child with a Disability

Children with disabilities face challenges in becoming independent, developing high levels of self-esteem, and getting along with peers. This section highlights how parents can help differently abled children achieve their fullest potential.

Needs of the Child with Disabilities

The differently abled child must be allowed to try. It may take him a long time to dress himself, but as he puts on his clothes, he is also raising his self-esteem. A child with braces does not have to be carried if his companions slow their pace to match his.

The differently abled child needs to be included. A child in a wheelchair may not be able to dance but he can join the circle and move his arms to the music.

The differently abled child needs to develop his strengths. A child whose legs don't work so well may be a fabulous singer. A child who can't express himself in words may be eloquent with paint. These talents are particularly important because they represent arenas in which the differently abled child can compete on an equal level with peers.

The differently abled child needs to develop a strong sense of identity. As he grows, he will encounter stereotypes, barriers, and prejudice. Society does not always make it easy for people who are different to participate in all aspects of life. He will need to be an advocate for himself. He will need to develop the confidence to say, "Give me a chance."

One of the building blocks of a strong personal identity is the knowledge that other people with disabilities have succeeded. This information can be communicated in a number of ways. The child will enjoy seeing television shows that include children with disabilities. He will relish books that depict physically challenged children functioning in a competent manner. He may want to own a doll with a disability. Playing with these dolls is also a great way for his able-bodied friends to achieve a greater level of comfort with disabilities. (See Resources for purchase information.)

The differently abled child needs to know how to handle questions about his condition. Each question represents an opportunity to demystify the subject of disabilities. Denying the differences or brushing off childrens' questions only adds to their fears. True understanding can only be achieved if misconceptions are addressed directly.

The child needs simple and accurate information. He needs to be able to assure other children that they will not "catch" his disability by playing with him. He should also, as part of his introduction, focus on the things he can do.

Children with disabilities need other services, such as special education, and physical, occupational, or speech therapy, to achieve their fullest potential. These services can be provided at no cost to the family through early intervention programs. These programs are supported by federal legislation that entitles all children to a free public education. The child's pediatrician is familiar with the local community's procedures for accessing services.

Children with disabilities have the same needs of autonomy, identity, and acceptance as their able-bodied peers. It is important not to allow their medical problems to overshadow these critical aspects of personality development.

Children, gifted, chronically ill, or physically challenged, have a few basic needs. They all need acceptance, support, and a chance to grow.

27

THE CHILD'S ROOM

The child's room is a multipurpose place. It is a play center, a stage, a tropical island, and a secret hideout. It is a home for games, art projects, and daydreams. At night it is transformed into a safe and secure setting for sleep. How can a room accommodate all these functions? This key provides some factors to consider when arranging a child's room.

A Child-Centered Space

In choosing furnishings, flexibility is an important asset. The key question to ask is, can this room grow with the child? The costly Cinderella's coach bed that was so cute when she was three may disgust her when she's eleven. Systems that can meet a child's changing needs for storage areas, shelves, and flat work surfaces are the best choice for a room that will be decorated only once.

Scale is an essential consideration in a child's room. In other areas of the house, the child must make do with furniture proportioned for adults. In her room, all the furniture should be child sized, except for a regular single bed.

A play table is a central element. It will be the site of tea parties, board games, science experiments, and art projects. Look for one with a strong surface impervious to crayon marks, glue, glitter, and magic marker. Make sure the table is of adequate size. Three year olds and their friends need a lot of room to work. If the table is too small, it will quickly become obsolete.

A comfortable table top for a three year old is 20 to 22 inches from the ground. Telescoping legs enhance a table's longevity. In choosing a chair, allow 8 to 10 inches clearance between the table top and the seat. Chair sizes are measured by the distance between the seat and the floor. Stackable chairs are ideal for a room with limited floorspace.

Floor and wall coverings should also be chosen with the knowledge that they will be exposed to paint, crayon, water, clay, and glue. Robust, easy to care for surfaces are best. Painted walls and vinyl floor tiles are enduring and washable.

A bulletin board is a good addition. It can be used to display artwork, photographs, postcards, and invitations. Other things to consider are a metal board for magnetic letters and numbers or a chalkboard.

A shatterproof mirror is handy in a child's room. One ingredient of a child's sense of self is an awareness of how she looks. For contrast, mount a piece of Mylar alongside the mirror. Mylar gives distorted images much the same way as a fun house mirror. A child delights in seeing herself grow tall and thin and then short and fat.

Active Play

Space for active play is a great advantage, especially on cold or rainy days. A gym mat or indoor trampoline provides an alternative to jumping on the couch. If the child's furniture is on casters, it can be easily moved to one side to make room for large muscle activities.

Quiet Play

Children also enjoy a cozy place where they can whisper with friends or retreat when they're in a bad mood. There are many ways to provide this. A tent that fits over the bed can be purchased. (See Resources.) A freestanding cardboard house is also an option. One can be bought or made from a large appliance box. Designing and decorating it can be a family project. Even a sheet draped over a table or a pair of chairs can supply the required degree of privacy.

Organization

The central question is how to organize the child's toys in a way that reduces clutter, minimizes lost objects, and ensures an easy cleanup. The most important principle is to have a home for each object. See-through bins or colored laundry baskets are ideal for storing the kinds of items a three year old collects. Remind her that the figurines belong in the purple basket, the blocks in the red basket, and the cars in the green basket. Bins can be labeled with a picture of the appropriate object. Larger toys and books can be placed on shelves labeled in a similar fashion. A pegboard can be used to store dress-up clothes or musical instruments. Trace an outline of the object in the space where it belongs. Putting the object away then becomes a game of matching the item and its shadow.

The options for storage are open shelves or cabinets with doors. There are advantages and disadvantages to both approaches. Cabinets reduce visual clutter. Beware of doors with hinges or drop leaves that can be dangerous to a young child. Sliding doors present fewer hazards but may be too heavy for a child to manipulate by herself.

The advantage to open shelves is that they are accessible. The child can reach her toys without help. The disadvantages are a cluttered appearance and the dumping syndrome. The dumping syndrome involves sweeping all the toys off the shelves and onto the floor. A visit from a young friend is usually the catalyst for the dumping syndrome.

One way to minimize the devastation is to limit the number of toys available at any one time. Prune her toy collection frequently. Leave out those she plays with frequently, and put the others away out of sight. When she gets bored, reintroduce one of her old toys. She will be as happy to see it as if it were a brand-new toy.

Three year olds cannot be counted on to clean up without help. They can learn certain routines that contribute to a neater home. Teach them to hang up their jackets as soon as they arrive home. If this routine is faithfully carried out, it soon becomes a reflex action. A coat rack or peg placed at their eye level enhances compliance.

There are strategies to make cleanup more fun. Put on some loud music and dance as the toys are put away. Set the timer, and promise the child a reward if the toys are back on the shelves before the bell rings. Parents don't need to do all the work. The trick is to put a few things away and then unobtrusively slow the pace and let the child do the major share. The parents' continued company and frequent praise keep the child on track.

A Room of Her Own

Not every child is able to have her own room. An alternative is to cordon off a small area that can serve as her private space. It can be set off from the rest of the room by a curtain or screen. Make sure that all members of the family know this is the child's space. Supply a shelf were she can store her toys, books, and other treasures. Allowing her to choose some pretty pictures from magazines or old calendars to tack on the wall is another way she can personalize her niche. The child's room does not need fancy furnishings to provide a safe, secure, and interesting place to be.

28

SAFETY

Mrs. Gold was babysitting for her three-year-old grandson, Jake, while his parents were out of town. They had been watching television together in her room. She stepped out for just a minute to take the cookies out of the oven. When she returned, she was horrified to see Jake happily munching on the pretty pink and white pills she took for her high blood pressure.

A ccidents claim the lives of more than 4,000 one- to four-year-old children in the United States each year. An awareness of the hazards in the child's environment can help save young lives.

Car Safety
Children should be secured into their seats for every ride. Car seats are suitable for children up to 40 pounds. For children who weigh more than 40 pounds, booster seats are recommended.

Booster seats position the child so that the lap-shoulder belt lies across the shoulder and not across the neck. The shoulder strap does not usually fit properly by itself until the child reaches a height of $4\frac{1}{2}$ feet. The other advantage of a booster seat is that it raises the child's vantage point, enabling him to see out the front window.

Parents sometimes place the ill-fitting shoulder portion of the belt behind the child's back rather than purchase a booster seat. This configuration compromises the effectiveness of the belt. It is safer to use a lap belt alone than a lap and shoulder belt with the shoulder portion behind the child.

Pedestrian Safety

Pedestrian safety rules are straightforward. Children quickly learn that they are supposed to cross at the corner after waiting for a green light or a walk signal. They know to reach for an adult's hand while crossing the street.

The real challenge is to apply these rules consistently. There is a real temptation, when parents are in a rush, to cross against the light when there is no traffic coming. For a young child who is trying to master the rules, inconsistent behavior is very confusing. It is much easier for him to learn rules that are absolute.

Playground Safety

Playground equipment should be checked for jagged edges, protruding screws, or exposed nuts or bolts that could injure children. Surfaces under swings or climbing apparatus should consist of soft grass, sand, or special safety padding. Children should be taught to cut a wide swath around swings to avoid being hit by them.

Water Safety

Children must be supervised at all times when they are in proximity to water. Even children who have had swimming lessons are not drownproof in an emergency. They should not be left alone even briefly while an adult goes to answer the phone or the door. Children can drown in a few inches of water. There have even been reports of children drowning in buckets.

Pools should be fenced and covered. Furniture that children can climb on to boost themselves over the fence should be moved away. Doors and windows that lead to the pool area should be equipped with a lock and an audible alarm system.

Safety equipment, such as a life preserver with a rope attached and a 10 foot pole, should be available at poolside. A telephone is also very useful. It obviates the need to run inside to make a quick call, and it is also helpful in an emergency. Post a list of emergency numbers so that help can be summoned quickly if needed.

Kitchen Safety

Children should be aware of the dangers of matches, open flames, cigarette lighters, and hot objects. Using the back burners on the stove reduces the risk of children being able to reach up and pull a hot pot down on themselves. Turning the pot handles to the side makes it more difficult for them to find something to grab.

Plastic bags pose a suffocation danger. They should be discarded promptly in a place that is not accessible to children.

Disconnect and store electrical appliances when they are not in use. This protects children from injury with such objects as grinders, mixers, and can openers.

Household Products

Household products should be stored in their original containers. Transferring the contents to soda bottles or other containers associated with food can be confusing to children.

Such products as insect sprays, kerosene, lighter fluid, some furniture polishes, turpentine, paint, solvents, and some cosmetics contain substances that can be dangerous if ingested by children. These products should be kept in locked cabinets separate from the ones used for food items.

Medicines should be left in the original bottles with the child-resistant caps. They should be stored in a locked cabinet.

Medications should not be left on counters, night tables, or dressers where children can reach them. Parents should be especially vigilant when they have guests or when they visit someone who does not ordinarily have children around.

Medicines should never be called candy in an effort to get children to take them without a fuss. Many ingestions occur because children mistake brightly colored and attractive pills for something good to eat. Old and outdated medications should be discarded.

Parents should be careful about the kinds of plants they have at home. Some plants have poisonous leaves or berries. Children sometimes eat the leaves of house plants while pretending to be animals or explorers stranded on a tropical island.

Children are fascinated by adult tools, such as scissors, knives, and drills. They cannot wait for a chance to use them. Children should practice with child-sized versions of these instruments. Tools should be locked away when not in use because of the temptation that they pose.

The same caution applies to guns. Guns kill 5,000 children in the United States each year. The average cost of treating a single child wounded by gunfire is more than $14,000. The best approach is not to store guns at home. If this is impossible, store the unloaded gun in a separate place from the ammunition.

A number of common household items pose choking hazards to young children. They include popcorn, hard candies, fruit pits, marbles, and coins. These objects should be kept out of children's reach. Children should be taught to sit, not run and play with food in their mouths. This also reduces the possibility of choking.

Smoke detectors should be installed near the family sleeping quarters.

Toy Safety

Parents should be cautious about toys that have sharp edges or propel objects that could injure the eyes. Arts and crafts materials should be clearly labeled "nontoxic." Costumes should be inflammable. Parents should check that wheel toys are well balanced. Children should only use electrical toys that need to be plugged into an outlet under the supervision of an adult.

Children should wear helmets, whether they are the pedaler or the passenger on a bicycle. The earlier that wearing a helmet becomes a habit, the less resistance there will be. Adults can set a good example by wearing theirs.

People Safety

Children need explicit rules about how to behave around strangers. They should be told never to accept food or treats from people they don't know. In public places, children should stay close to their companions. They should never walk away with a stranger or enter a stranger's car.

Children should be warned that strangers often employ very cunning tactics. They may tell the child that his parents are hurt or ill and want him to come with them. They may try to enlist the child's aid in locating a lost pet.

Children should also know that their bodies are private. No one has the right to touch their genitals except in a medical or caretaking context. Children should be informed that they have the right to say "no" to any requests that make them feel bad or uncomfortable. Children should be encouraged to tell their parents if anyone is hurting them or asking them to do things against their will.

These precautions are not intended to make a child fearful. The underlying theme of the discussion is reassurance. Parents are conveying their desire to protect the child and keep him safe.

Pet Safety

Children generally love animals, and proper pet safety ensures that this relationship will flourish. Children should be taught to approach all unfamiliar animals with caution. Check with the owner before attempting to pet an animal. Teach children to stand still and allow the animal to sniff and observe them before moving to touch it. Children should be particularly careful with animals that are eating, sleeping, or minding their young.

Most safety rules reflect common sense. Following them will reduce senseless death and injury.

29

CHOOSING A
PRESCHOOL

*The visit to the Decatur Preschool had gone well. Much
to Mr. and Mrs. Nemir's surprise, Annie had separated easily
from them. She accompanied the admissions director to her
office for 15 long minutes. When Annie emerged, she was
beaming and carrying a large envelope of stickers. Then she
and the admissions director trotted off hand in hand for a
look at the classroom.*

*When Annie returned, Mr. Nemir reached up to remove
his daughter's jacket from the coat rack. Annie was not ready
to give up her newly acquired student status, however. She
glared at the admissions director and burst into tears. "I don't
like this place and I don't like you," she sobbed.*

Sending a child to preschool is a significant milestone in
the life of a family. Parents are now sharing their child
with a wider world. They wonder how she will represent
their ideas, beliefs, and values. There are other questions as
well. Will she be a successful learner? Will she make friends?
Will she be happy?

Parents want to find a place where their child will thrive
and be successful, but how do they find a school that will both
nurture and challenge the young learner? What are the important features of a quality program? This key provides answers
to these important questions.

Great Expectations

Parents must be clear about the goals of a preschool education. The role of a preschool is to help the child find out about her feelings, her ideas, her abilities, and her self. She learns how to think, but also how to make friends, share, take turns, move through space, work in a group, follow classroom routines, and interact with adults outside her family. The initial school experience should leave her enthusiastic, curious, and confident about her ability to learn. It is not designed to put her on the fast track to academic achievement. A child exposed to formal lessons too early often finds herself anxious and bored.

Classroom and Curriculum

Young children learn by doing. They need to squash the clay, climb to the top of the slide, drizzle glue on their hands, and try on the high-heeled shoes. They need an environment that is stimulating but not chaotic; challenging while nurturing; free yet secure.

Preschool classrooms are usually divided into various interest areas: blocks, dress-up, art, books, games, and puzzles. Activities should be flexible enough to be enjoyed by children of differing ability levels and attention spans. While participating in these activities, children learn to express themselves, make choices, and have an impact on their environment. Dress-up provides an opportunity to develop language and imagination. A child tries on adult roles as she tries on adult clothes. Art activities allow a child to represent relationships between objects. She makes decisions about what colors to use and where to place them on the paper. Dance teaches about space, shape, balance, and sequence. Fine motor skills are developed through the use of blocks, pegs, tools, and puzzles. Through music a child can enhance language skills, create a new song, and appreciate the cultures of other people.

The Daily Schedule

A look at the daily schedule can be very informative. Is there a balance between quiet and active, individual and group, free choice and mandatory, indoor and outdoor, and new and familiar activities? How long are the activity periods? Is enough time alloted for projects to be completed? Is there time scheduled for cleanup? How are the transitions between activities handled? Is there something for the early finishers to do while waiting for the others to join them? Are there special events in the calendar? A neighborhood walking trip or a cooking project can really enliven the curriculum.

Spending some time in the classroom can help parents in their decision making. Observation at morning dropoff time can be particularly revealing. Does the teacher greet the children in a positive way? Do the children have a set routine that they seem to understand and follow? How does the teacher acknowledge the parents? How does the teacher intervene with children who seem reluctant to separate from their parents?

Observe a classroom activity. Do the children seem involved, or are some wandering aimlessly through the classroom? Are they having fun? Are they relating to one another? How does the teacher respond to the children's work?

The physical environment must be evaluated from the child's perspective. Is the room attractive? Are materials at the child's eye level? Are decorations placed where a child can see them? Are there sufficient numbers of interesting toys? Is the room arranged so that the teacher can see all the children?

Safety is another critical aspect. Look for smoke detectors in the rooms. Make sure that cleaning fluids are stored out of reach. Special safety surfaces should be under and around outdoor play equipment. Emergency numbers should be clearly posted next to the telephone. Ask the staff how emergencies are handled. A clear plan indicates a school that is well run.

Staff

Relationships with the staff play a major role in satisfaction with a school. A program for three year olds should ideally have one teacher and one assistant for 16 children. Find out how long the teacher has been working at the school. High staff turnover may reflect internal problems.

Another point to investigate is how teachers share feedback about the children with the parents. Are there conferences or newletters? Are the teachers available to chat informally with the parents at pickup and dropoff time? Can the teachers be reached by telephone in the evenings? Do they seem interested in learning about the children's home environments? Does the teacher encourage parental involvement in the classroom? Are parents free to visit at any time?

Parents should also find out about disciplinary practices. Are children guided in a positive way, or are they yelled at or punished? How does the staff handle children who are disruptive?

A Good Match

Fantastic facilities and a top-flight staff are not the only considerations. There must be a good match between the personality of the child and the personality of the school. An active child needs a place for large motor activity every day. A cozy, private spot is a must for a child who is overwhelmed easily. A child who is slow to warm up may need to have a parent in the classroom for the first week or two until she becomes adjusted. One child may thrive in a structured setting; another does better in a situation that is more flexible.

The child's initial exposure to preschool sets the tone for her future academic career. Attention to the factors mentioned in this key will ensure a good fit between student and school.

30

THE BIRTHDAY PARTY

6:00 A.M. Sebastian jumped into his parents' bed. "It's my birthday!" he announced joyfully. He eyed the colorfully wrapped packages stacked in the corner. "Would you like to open your presents now?" his mother asked. Sebastian eagerly applied himself to the task.

8:00 A.M. The balloons were blown up and the crepe paper streamers were tacked to the walls. Mr. Forsyte wondered how they would keep the decorations intact until the guests arrived.

4:00 P.M. The last guest was escorted to the door. Sebastian was in his room surrounded by three new teddy bears of various sizes. An aunt had been dispatched to the store to pick up batteries. The living room floor was strewn with bits of colored paper and cake crumbs. A puddle of apple juice swelled on the table. It had been a full and exhausting day, but making it special for Sebastian was worth it.

A birthday celebration need not be elaborate to be special. The memories a child treasures are the feelings of being loved and honored by his family. This is a time to develop meaningful traditions that reflect the family's values.

There are many ways to make a child feel special. One way is to allow him to be the boss for the day. Let him suggest the menu for the birthday meal. Find out whether he'd rather spend the day at the beach or at the zoo.

To Party or Not to Party

Some families choose to spend the day with close relatives or friends. By the time a child goes to nursery school, he is likely to want a celebration that includes his friends. A horde of three year olds can be overwhelming. A sensible rule for children's parties is that the number of young guests should equal the birthday child's age plus one. This limitation may not be possible if the child's school adheres to an invite the whole class party policy.

Pick a theme for the party. The theme of the party should relate to the child's interests. Sebastian, who loved teddy bears, had a bearthday party. Each party goer was invited to bring his favorite stuffed animal to the festivities. The hosts of the party have the option of dressing in keeping with the theme. One mother, for instance, wore a hula skirt to her daughter's Hawaiian party.

A key hint is to keep the party short. One and a half hours is plenty of time for a social gathering of three year olds.

Another important tip is to plan enough activities. Three year olds have short attention spans. In addition, sometimes a game that seemed great in the party book turns out to be a dud at the actual party. Plan a special activity to amuse the early arrivals while the rest of the group is assembling. The children can design a birthday mural with crayons and paper or simply dance to music.

Expect that many of the parents will stay for the party. Three year olds may be reluctant to separate from their parents, particularly in an unfamiliar environment. Having several extra pairs of hands is a boon when it is time to pour juice or mop up spills.

Having the parents on hand is also useful when social problems arise. A shy child may linger on the outskirts of the group and refuse to participate in the activities. A parent can stay with him and keep him from being lonely until he warms up.

Another child may want to find out how jumping on the couch is regarded at his friend's house. His parent can quickly step in to set limits.

High-excitement times like parties are reliable triggers for tears. Not everyone can sit next to the birthday child. It is not unusual for the birthday child himself to fall apart under the pressure of being the center of attention. Extra parents are ideal for soothing the bruised feelings of the young guests.

Refreshments

Keep the food simple. Remember that once the children are seated their attention spans may be quite short. Treats like cupcakes are ideal. They don't require utensils, can be handed out quickly, and come in only one size. This eliminates the complaints about who got the bigger slice of cake or the extra dollop of frosting.

Young children are bewildered by too many choices. A choice of milk or juice should provide a beverage acceptable to almost everyone. One flavor of cake, with an alternative for anyone who's allergic, should suffice.

Favors

If party favors are to be given out, distribute them at the door once the guests are dressed and ready to leave. Make sure that the party bags are sealed. This eliminates spillage and last-minute complaints that Lamar got more candy or that Sonia didn't get a red lollypop.

Presenting the Presents

Opening the presents is a classic party tradition, but it is not a good activity for three year olds. Three year olds still do not fully understand the intricacies of sharing and ownership. The guests have difficulty sitting by and watching one child unwrap a multitude of toys. It is a tease to reveal an attractive toy and then not be able to play with it. The sheer volume of many new playthings in a single day can overwhelm the birthday child and diminish his appreciation.

This is an excellent time to establish the one-gift-a-day tradition. The child can start by opening the gift from his parents on his birthday. From then on, he selects a single gift to open each day for as long as the packages last. This approach allows the child really to focus on and appreciate each gift individually. It also prolongs the fun.

Memories, Photos, and Videotape

Children grow up very fast. Mementos of their birthdays and other special events are invaluable. Appoint a responsible, knowledgeable, and willing person to serve as cameraperson at the party.

Some families have a birthday ritual of taking a photograph of the child in the same setting each year. Other families prefer to have an annual group picture taken on this special day.

The best birthday celebration is the one that makes the child feel appreciated and special. Love is the most important birthday present of all.

31

~~~~~~

TRAVELING

The children were arguing over the use of the armrest. They paused only long enough to ask, "Are we there yet?" Mrs. Kirkland was fed up with fast food. Mr. Kirkland didn't think visiting his in-laws was much of a vacation anyway. Why had they ever left home?

Parents who have fond memories of traveling look forward to taking their children on trips. It is a chance to try out a new environment, to learn, to relax, and to socialize. A three year old can be a challenging travel companion. This key has some tips on trips.

Realistic Expectations

The three museum, four cathedral a day itinerary is unrealistic for young children. They cannot keep up a blistering and unrelenting pace. Packing in a lot of activity is difficult because everything takes longer with children in tow. A too ambitious itinerary that can never be completed can leave everyone feeling tense and frustrated.

A useful strategy is to schedule the most ambitious destination for the children's most energetic time of the day. For most children, this is the first thing in the morning. Look particularly for museums that have specially designed hands-on exhibits for young visitors.

Plans must accommodate a child's variable attention span. A walk through the park may take longer than anticipated because he stops to take a sample from every water fountain. The leisurely afternoon at the sidewalk cafe may have to be cut short when he gets bored.

Plan frequent breaks during the day so that the child does not become tired, hungry, and grouchy. A child's fondest memory of a trip may be stopping at a park to feed the ducks or sitting on a bench eating pistachio ice cream. Make sure there is time for regular activities, such as playing in the playground, swimming, and lounging around. An advantage to frequenting the playground is the opportunity it affords to meet other parents. They know the best pizza parlors in town and countless other places to go with children that are not mentioned in any guidebook.

Security Blankets

Children's behavior may deteriorate when they are away from home. It can be hard for them to function without the security of familiar household objects and routines. There are several areas in which parents can provide a much needed sense of consistency.

One key area is eating. On a trip, a child may be exposed to many new foods. He may eat in restaurants or other people's homes more frequently than he would ordinarily. Eating once in a while in the local branch of a familiar restaurant chain can be a big relief.

Bedtime is another important anchor in the day. During a vacation, the child may be allowed to stay up later than he would at home. His nap may be forgotten in the rush of a hectic afternoon. Increased activity combined with less sleep can result in an irritable child. It is important that the traveling child get an adequate amount of sleep. Reconstructing his bedtime routine helps him relax and fall asleep at night. A night-light will illuminate the murky corners of an unfamiliar room.

Packing some familiar objects from home also helps. These may include the child's favorite stuffed animal, special blanket, books, or small toys. Have the child sit by while his suitcase is being packed. Ask him to choose which sweater or bathing suit to take. When he sees these items unpacked at the destination, he experiences a welcome sense of reunion.

Sibling rivalry may also escalate on a trip. Children who may not spend much time together at home suddenly become constant companions in cramped quarters. One way to deal with this is to separate the children occasionally. Perhaps an older child would enjoy visiting a museum with one parent while the younger child goes to the playground. This provides a nice opportunity for a parent to have some one-on-one interaction with the child.

Planes, Trains, and Automobiles

Air travel is a quick and convenient way for families to reach their destinations. Try to book a direct flight if one is available. Many families prefer seating in the bulkhead area because of its increased leg room.

The contents of the carry-on bag are key in making the flight a pleasant experience. One essential item is gum. Changing air pressure in the cabin can cause ear pain. Chewing gum during the ascent and descent helps children equalize the air pressure in their ears, thus avoiding ear pain. If the child is too young to chew gum, instruct him to swallow repeatedly or take some sips of juice.

It is also a good idea to bring along some snacks. Some airlines offer special children's meals, which may be more appealing than the food served to adults. These meals must usually be ordered in advance.

Books, cassette tapes, and card games all help stave off boredom during the ride. A new toy also gets a lot of mileage. The carry-on bag should include a change of clothes and other necessities in case the luggage gets lost. If the child's car seat is approved for air travel, it provides a safer ride than the regular seat with seat belt.

Train travel is well suited to families with young children. It is more economical than travel by air. A great advantage is that the young train traveler can walk around when he becomes restless.

Many of the hints that combat boredom on a plane apply equally well to travel by car. When the child becomes tired of looking out the window, he may fall asleep. Providing him with a small pillow makes him more comfortable. A child who becomes car sick may feel better riding up front, where he can look out on the horizon. Plan frequent breaks to see local sights or just to get some exercise. Cover the car seat with a towel when the car is parked in the sun. This way the buckles are not too hot to use when the child returns to the car. A string bag draped over the seat in front of him is an ideal receptacle for the child's toys, tapes, and empty juice boxes.

A well-stocked emergency kit comes in handy when minor medical problems arise and reduces the need for middle-of-the-night pharmacy runs in unfamiliar locations. The kit should contain a cold pack, bandages, antiseptic, tweezers, scissors, calamine lotion, acetaminophen, antihistamine, ipecac, a measuring spoon, and a thermometer. Families should also bring their medical insurance cards and a listing of allergies and current medications. An extra signed prescription form hastens the replacement of any medication that is lost or left behind.

When Parents Travel

Sometimes the parents take a trip without the child. It is important to let the child know in advance. Because young children have a poorly developed sense of time, telling them a few days before departure is sufficient. Be sure to mention where they will stay and and who will take care of them.

There are many ways parents can maintain contact while they travel. A child loves to receive mail. It is ideal for him to get a card or a letter daily. Parents can leave a stash with the child's caretaker to ensure that he gets something the day after their departure. If the child likes to talk on the telephone, a daily call can be comforting. Some parents leave a gift for the child to open after they leave.

Parents can leave audio or video recordings for the child to use while they are away. A tape recording of a favorite song or story can be incorporated into the bedtime routine.

The child will be very interested in knowing when the parents are due back. One simple way to convey this is to assemble a booklet with one page for each day of the trip. The child tears off a page each night until Mom and Dad return. This is a lot easier for a young child than the traditional calendar.

Traveling with young children can be an enriching experience if parents are willing to take a relaxed approach. Bon voyage!

32

MOVING DAY

Amy was 3½ when the Lewis family moved. Their new apartment was in a different neighborhood in the same city. The Lewises visited there several times. Amy inspected her new room and the backyard. Her favorite part of the house was the playroom, which had space for a kitchen set with a sink and an oven. They also stopped by the playground and the nursery school where Amy would be going in the fall.

Finally, the big day arrived. After all their belongings had been packed in the truck, Amy and her mother set off by car for their new home. By the time they pulled up in front, Amy was crying hysterically and refused to get out of the car.

Moving, even to a more comfortable home, can pose problems for a young child. Moving means a disruption of familiar patterns and associations. Even if the new home has the advantages of a bigger bedroom or a grassy backyard, the initial adjustment can be difficult. This key details the ways in which parents can help a child who is facing a move.

The Importance of Patterns

A young child learns through patterns. Routines help her make sense of the complexities of daily life. There is the morning routine of waking, getting dressed, and having breakfast. The nightly ritual involves a bath and a bedtime story.

Patterns develop around the child's physical world as well. She learns where the kitchen is in relation to her room. She knows which direction takes her to the supermarket and which leads to the park. Moving disrupts all these established patterns, which is why it can be so stressful.

Before the Move

Parental intervention should center on minimizing disruptions and helping the child establish new patterns.

Parents should begin by discussing the reasons for the move. Children will be attentive, not only to the facts, but to their parents' attitudes. If the parents are positive about the move, the children will be, too.

Parents can also be honest about any reservations they have. Children are comforted to know that their parents share their feelings about missing friends and neighborhood haunts.

Children need extra attention during this period. Seeing their parents preoccupied with the details of moving can make them feel isolated and frightened. It is preferable if the bulk of packing can be done at night after the children are asleep.

The child can participate by packing a few of her most treasured possessions in a specially marked box. This box should accompany her to the new house. Unpacking her special box can occupy the child while the parents are busy with the movers.

Moving may feature prominently in the child's play. She is trying to understand the concept of moving as she piles up her toys on her wagon and unloads them at a distant place. Parents can support this type of play by providing boxes, tape, and bubble wrap.

Many excellent children's books deal with the topic of moving. The child is glad to know that other children have also faced this stress. The books depict models for coping that may prove helpful in her situation. Recommended titles appear in Books for Children.

Visiting the new home as often as possible before the move is important. This allows the child to become familiar with the new layout and create her own mental map of the place. Spend a night in the new apartment to get used to the ambient sounds. If the furniture is not yet in place, sleeping bags can make this a great adventure. If the new home is too far away to visit, be sure to provide the child with photographs of the house, park, school, and other neighborhood landmarks.

The New Room

Let the child know which room will be hers. She will feel more connected to her new room if she is allowed to pick out something simple to go in it. Parents may also decide to purchase a longed-for toy, like Amy's kitchen set, and place it in the new room. Some of the initial strangeness can be lessened if the new room is initially set up similarly to the old room. If the arrangement must be changed, this can be done later, once the child has adjusted.

Moving Day

Even a well-prepared child can be easily upset on moving day. Seeing the house being emptied can bother her. Much of the child's identity is connected to her possessions. Bare walls and empty rooms lack the character associated with home. Reassure her that all the family's belongings will be taken and that nothing will be lost in the transfer.

Parents should arrange for the child's things to be the last on the moving truck. This means that the child's room remains

159

intact for the longest time. It also assures that the child's furniture is the most accessible at the destination. The child's room should be set up first. Seeing her familiar things again will contribute greatly to the child's feeling settled and secure.

If the trip to the new home is a long one, plan a stop along the way. Make sure that the child gets to do something enjoyable and familiar, such as play in the park.

Children may show behavioral changes following a move. There may be an increase in clinging or the development of sleep problems. These changes are normal and tend to resolve within a few weeks.

Temporary Housing

Many children live in temporary housing with relatives or in shelters. Sometimes they must move frequently before a permanent home is found. In this situation parents must emphasize that although their surroundings may change, their bonds as a family are enduring. Possessions with a history take on a special importance. A quilt or a stuffed animal that has been through every move symbolizes home. Parents must make sure that these treasured items figure prominently even in the most temporary of situations.

Follow-up

Mrs. Lewis picked up her crying daughter and carried her into the house. Amy could not be distracted even by her beloved kitchen set. Because the moving truck had not yet arrived, Mrs. Lewis and Amy went to explore the local playground. Several months later, the family walked past their old building and Amy did not even show a flicker of recognition.

33

PEOPLE WITH
DIFFERENCES

"Why does that man have such a big nose?" asked Nicky loudly. Everyone in the crowded department store elevator turned around to better hear Nicky's mother's reply. "It's not polite to ask," she muttered through clenched teeth. When the elevator door opened, she yanked him out even though it was not their floor.

Young children are quick to notice differences among people. Being observant is a good thing. It is the way that children gather information about their world. Once children have this information, they look to trusted adults for help in putting it into context. This is a critical step. The attitudes that are acquired in childhood last a lifetime.

Understanding Differences

The child's thinking abilities influence the way he understands differences. A three year old is in the preoperational stage of cognitive development. (See also Key 4.) For a preoperational child, physical differences are salient. He divides people into groups based on a single visual attribute. His groups consist, for instance, of all people with short hair or all people who wear pants. He does not understand that groupings based on superficial characteristics are not really the most meaningful.

A three year old's categories tend to be rigid and exclusive. He lacks the mental flexibility to think about more than one attribute at a time. A person is either a man or a woman. A person has either short hair or long hair. He does not see how people who are dissimilar in one dimension could be similar in another. His framework cannot account for the fact that both men and women can have short hair.

By age three, children notice differences in gender, color, and other physical abilities. They are aware of men and women, light skin and dark skin, glasses, and hearing aids. The next step involves learning the difference between intrinsic and superficial characteristics. They begin to understand that a person's sex is not determined by hair, wardrobe, or career choice. A change in hair length can occur without a change in gender. They also learn which features are permanent and which are subject to change. A dark-skinned person cannot change his or her skin color by scrubbing harder during the morning shower.

In addition to information, a child picks up attitudes. Parents are an enormous influence in this process. A child is very sensitive to his parents' views. If a parent says disparaging things about a group of people, the child echoes these sentiments.

A child also learns from his own experience. Playing with children from different backgrounds is extremely effective in countering stereotypes. Books, toys, television shows, and videos are very important. They can reinforce negative images, or they can provide strong role models. Parents can use the power of the media to bring diversity and pride to a child's world.

Dealing with Bias

Bias hurts all children. It limits the expression of talent and, as a result, makes the world a far poorer place. It is not healthy for a girl to be told she cannot be a scientist. An African-American child needs role models besides rap singers and basketball players. Children with disabilities can contribute when they have the opportunity for full participation.

Bias can be countered by dealing with children's questions. These queries must be answered honestly. Stereotypes must be confronted and contradicted. Ignoring difficult issues does not make them go away. The curiosity is merely turned inward, where it feeds misconceptions and fears.

There are occasions when the timing of questions is less than ideal. One option is to say to the child, "We will talk about this when we get home." A child can be instructed to whisper observations regarding a person's appearance to avoid hurting someone's feelings.

Bigoted language must be dealt with directly. Sometimes the child is imitating words he has heard with no understanding of their offensive meaning. Parents must explain that racial epithets hurt peoples' feelings and are not acceptable.

Parents must also be aware of the examples they set. Do they introduce their children to a diversity of people, if not in person then through books and television? Are they consistently respectful toward others? Do they actively reject group stereotypes? Do they provide equal support for their sons and daughters, or are boys noticed for their work and girls for their appearance?

Efforts to counteract bias must start when children are young. The best approach is to make sure that children have opportunities to interact with children from various cultural, ethnic, and racial groups. Prejudice cannot take hold in an atmosphere of cooperation and inclusion. Children who know a wide range of people develop empathy rather than a false sense of superiority. They learn to identify with the world as a whole.

Children are not born color-blind. They notice differences and ask questions. Each question represents an opportunity to educate a more open, accepting, and caring citizen of the world.

QUESTIONS AND ANSWERS

My three year old always wreaks havoc while I'm on the telephone. What can I do?

A three year old wants to be in the spotlight all the time. When you are on the telephone, you are occupied with someone else. The child counters by doing something provocative to regain your attention.

You need to find a balance between concentrating on the phone conversation and tending to the child. One strategy is to keep the child within view. Sometimes a withering glance can quell incipient mischievous behavior. Allow him to play at your feet with a toy or a book. Give him an important job to do, such as folding the laundry or setting the table.

The reality is that phone conversations must to be limited while the child is up and about. Let the child know that the call is important and that you will be with him shortly. Set a kitchen timer for five minutes, and wind up the conversation promptly when the bell rings. Save the long chats for times when the child is asleep or out of the house.

Should I try to let my child win when we play games? I want him to grow up with a strong self-concept.

It is not necessary for children to win all the time at games. One of the purposes in playing, in fact, is to learn to be a good sport. Win or lose, children need to be gracious, fair, and cooperative. They have an opportunity to practice these responses when they first start to play games at home. The supportive home environment can cushion a defeat or place a win into perspective. The emphasis in game playing should be on having fun. The gains in self-esteem come from an enjoyable interaction with a responsive partner, not from a 10 game winning streak.

My three-year-old daughter has been playing doctor with the three-year-old boy next door. Should I be concerned about this?

Three year olds have a natural curiosity about the differences in anatomy between boys and girls. Playing doctor is one way for them to explore this interest.

The best response is to handle the situation matter-of-factly. Acknowledge that there are interesting differences between boys' and girls' bodies. This statement gives children permission to ask further questions at a more opportune time. Help the children get dressed, and assist them in getting started on a new game.

A calm reaction is key. Overreacting may suppress exploratory behavior but does not eliminate the curiosity. Overly permissive attitudes expose children to sexual situations before they are emotionally ready to handle them.

I would like my three year old to attend the birth of his sibling. Some of my friends don't think this is a good idea. What are some of the advantages and disadvantages?

A well-prepared three year old may be able to handle an easy birth, but there is no way to guarantee that the birth will be easy. A three year old is not emotionally equipped to see his treasured mother in pain and out of control. He may also be frightened by the blood, which is something he associates with hurt and injury.

A compromise for families who really want the three year old to be part of the birth process is to have him stay with a close friend during labor and bring him in either for the actual birth or immediately thereafter. Parents should make sure that the child knows exactly what will occur. A person must be available to remove the child if he becomes overwhelmed or scared.

I don't feel that my three year old speaks as well as other children his age. A friend told me that Einstein didn't speak until he was six. Should I do something now or wait for my son to outgrow this problem?

The vast majority of language development takes place early in life. Linguists report that 80% of language learning occurs by age three. It is important to address language problems promptly so that help can be provided during this fertile learning period.

Share your concerns with the child's pediatrician. He or she can set up a formal evaluation of your child's language development. A hearing test may also be included. If a problem is detected, your son can be started in speech therapy. If your son's language development is found to be normal for age, your concerns will be allayed.

It takes a lot of courage to acknowledge that there might be a problem with your child. It is in your son's best interest to investigate your suspicions promptly and provide him with any needed help.

My three-year-old son wants to play with dolls. Should I let him?

Yes. All children should be exposed to a wide variety of play materials. Boys need to develop their nurturing sides just as girls need to become comfortable with tools and baseball mitts. At three, children need to know that life provides many options. Parents can help by supporting their interests.

My three year old can write his name, the letters of the alphabet, and numbers up to 10. He can even read some simple words. Is he gifted?

Maybe. Gifted children may exhibit any one of a number of talents, from exemplary athletic prowess to intellectual advancement. The most important thing that parents of a bright young child can do is support his interests. Read books with him, and discuss the events and the characters. Let him learn by doing and seeing. A walk around the neighborhood is far more stimulating than a session with a workbook. Don't push him. A child needs to feel valued for who he is rather than what he can do. Keep up with age-appropriate limits. Although he may be intellectually advanced, emotionally he is still a three-year-old child.

I've tried time-out, but my child just bolts from the chair. What should I do?

The child needs to spend the entire interval in the time-out location. Parents must return the child to time-out when he runs off. It is important to return the child calmly and quietly so that it doesn't seem like a game. If the child runs off more than twice, holding may be in order. Hold him in the chair by pressing his shoulders down from behind. Explain that you will stop holding him when he is able to sit quietly by himself. If you apply this strategy consistently, he should be able to maintain himself within a week.

What should I tell my three year old about strangers? I don't want to scare her, but I want her to be informed.

Rules about strangers should be conveyed to young children and reviewed with them frequently.

Children should be told never to accept food or treats from strangers. They should never walk off with a stranger or enter a stranger's car. Children should be aware that strangers often use very cunning schemes. They may tell a child that her parents are ill or hurt and want her to come with them. They may try to elicit the child's help in searching for a lost pet.

Children should also know that no one has the right to touch their genitals. The only exceptions are in the context of caretaking or medical examinations.

My three-year-old son constantly hits his younger brother. What can I do about his aggressive behavior?

It is important at this age to distinguish between aggressive and assertive behavior.

A child is being assertive when he attempts to get his needs met in a direct way. For instance, he may grab a toy from his sibling, accidentally knocking the younger child down in the process.

An aggressive child, however, acts without regard for the feelings, rights, possessions, or safety of others. In assessing aggressive behavior, it is critical to document its frequency and the number of settings in which it occurs. Recurrent aggressive acts that happen both at home and at school are more worrisome than a few isolated incidents. A child who always seems angry or anxious may have a more serious problem than one who is generally positive and upbeat in outlook. It is also necessary to look at the home environment. A child who witnesses or experiences violent behavior at home is more likely to respond aggressively when faced with a conflict.

GLOSSARY

Amblyopia condition in which vision in one eye is better than vision in the other eye. It results in suppression of the vision in the stronger eye.

Anemia decrease in the amount of red cells in the blood.

Animism process of endowing inanimate objects with characteristics of living things.

Cholesterol fatty substance in the blood responsible for narrowing of blood vessels.

Cognitive development unfolding of thinking and learning capacities.

Concrete thinking mental processes dominated by what one can see and experience directly.

Cyanotic blue discoloration of the skin caused by low oxygen levels in the blood.

Diuretic medication that helps the body get rid of excess fluid.

Dysfluency speech problem consisting of repetition of syllables, words, or phrases.

Egocentric feeling of one's self as the center of the universe.

Encopresis involuntary passage of feces.

Enuresis bed-wetting.

Expressive language language that the child produces himself.

Occupational therapy remediation focusing on the small muscle groups.

Ophthalmologist physician specializing in the care of the eyes.

Physical therapy remediation through exercises aimed at the large muscles of the body.

PPD (purified protein derivative) skin test for tuberculosis.

Receptive language what the child understands when spoken to by others.

Regression loss of developmental milestones. Often occurs in response to stress.

Strabismus crossed eyes.

Stuttering synonym of dysfluency.

Tympanogram examination that measures pressure in the middle ear. It can indicate the presence of fluid from an unresolved ear infection. It is not a hearing test.

RESOURCES

Adoption

Ours, the Magazine of Adoptive Families
(612) 535-4829

Attention Deficit Disorder

Children and Adults with Attention Deficit Disorders (CHADD)
499 N.W. 70 Avenue, Suite 109
Plantation, FL 33137
(305) 587-3700

Child Care

Child Care Aware National Referral source for child care.
(800) 424-2246

Children of Color

National Black Child Development Institute
Advocacy group for black children and youth.
(202) 387-1281

Children's Furnishings (Bed Tents)

Childcraft catalog
(800) 631-5652
Right Start catalog
(800) 548-8531

Divorce

K.I.D.S. Express!
P.O. Box 782
Littleton, CO 80160-0782
Monthly newsletter for children about divorce.

Dolls

Hal's Pals
P.O. Box 3490
Winter Park, CO 80482
(303) 726-8388
Source for dolls with disabilities.

Fathers

Full-Time Dads
P.O. Box 577
Cumberland, ME 04021
Newsletter for fathers who are primary caretakers.

Gifted Children

American Association for Gifted Children
1121 West Main Street, Suite 100
Durham, NC 27705
Publishes a quarterly newsletter. Parents may request a free copy.

Grandparents

Foundation for Grandparenting
P.O. Box 326
Cohasset, MA 02025
Publishes a newsletter and runs a summer camp.

Hearing Impaired

American Speech-Language-Hearing Association
(800) 638-8255 (voice, TDD)
Brochures available on hearing and speech topics.

Nature

National Wildlife Federation
1400 16 Street, N.W.
Washington, D.C. 20036-2266
(800) 432-6564
Publishes *Your Big Backyard,* a magazine for animal-loving children.

Safety

Safety Belt Safe USA
(800) 745-SAFE
Information source on child passenger safety issues.

Consumer Product Safety Commission
(800) 638-2772
Hotline offers toy safety information.

ACTIVITY BOOKS FOR ADULTS

Brashears, Deya. *Dribble Drabble*. A collection of engaging art activities.

Brown, Sam Ed. *Bubbles, Rainbows & Worms*. Science-oriented activities focusing on air, animals, and the environment.

Bove, Linda. *Sign Language ABC*. Children's Television Workshop. Finger-spelled alphabet and simple signs depicted in easy-to-follow photographs.

Cromwell, Liz, and Dixie Hibner. *Finger Frolics*. Poems and rhymes with accompanying hand movements.

Gilbert, La Britta. *Do Touch*. Activities using common household objects.

James, J., and R. Granovetter. *Waterworks*. Children love nothing better than water play.

Kohl, Mary Ann F. *Mudworks*. Recipes for play doughs, edible doughs, and other molding mixtures.

Kohl, Mary Ann F. *Scribble Cookies*. Wonderful, original art activities.

Kohl, Mary Ann F., and Jean Potjer. *ScienceArts*. Combination science-art activities classified by season and level of difficulty.

Linderman, Emma C. *Teachables from Trashables*. Recycle junk into toys.

Rockwell, R., E. Sherwood, and R. Williams. *Hug a Tree*. Outdoor adventures for young children.

Stavros, S., and L. Peters. *Big Learning for Little Learners*. Over 500 learning activities.

Stangl, J. *Magic Mixtures*. Simple doughs and clays to make at home.

Williams, R., R. Rockwell, and E. Sherwood. *Mudpies to Magnets*. Fascinating, hands-on science experiments using easy to obtain materials.

VIDEOS FOR CHILDREN

Big Rigs. A truck-lover's delight: different types of trucks unencumbered by narration. Chinaberry, (800) 776-2242.

Choo Choo Trains. A train-lover's version of *Big Rigs.* Chinaberry, (800) 776-2242.

Corduroy and Other Bear Stories. Children's Circle Home Video. Charming animations of three classic bear stories.

Critter Hunt. Accompany a biologist on a pond expedition without getting wet. Chinaberry, (800) 776-2242.

Farm Animals. Low-key video that is like a visit to a barnyard. Chinaberry, (800) 776-2242.

Sesame Street's a New Baby in My House. Sesame Street characters share life with a younger sibling. Includes parent guide featuring tips and activities.

AUDIO FOR CHILDREN

Bartels, Joanie. *Sillytime Magic.* Classics performed with spunk and energy.

Chapin, Tom. *Family Tree.* There's a wonderful sense of fun that pervades these original tunes.

Henson, Jim. *A Sesame Street Celebration.* Collection includes "Rubber Duckie" and the "African Alphabet" song.

Paxton, Tom. *The Marvelous Toy.* Original songs that are appealing in their simplicity and humor.

Pease, Tom. *Boogie! Boogie! Boogie!* Upbeat collection of songs featuring varied instrumentation and a children's chorus.

Raposo, Joe. *Sesame Street Sing.* Classic songs with lyrics included.

Sharon, Lois, and Bram Sing A to Z. Lullabies, spelling songs, and nonsense tunes from many nations.

Shih, Patricia. *Big Ideas!* Original songs with positive messages.

BOOKS FOR
CHILDREN

Adoption

Caines, J. *Abby*. A story about adoption.

Death

de Paolo, T. *Nana Upstairs and Nana Downstairs*. A child experiences the deaths of his two grandmothers.

Wilhelm, H. *I'll Always Love You*. A touching story about a boy coping with the death of his pet.

Family Issues

Adoff, A. *Black Is Brown Is Tan*. Different shades of skin color within a family.

Alexander, M. *Nobody Asked Me if I Wanted a Baby Sister.*
When the New Baby Comes, I'm Moving Out.

The child's voice really rings true in these two stories depicting an older sibling and a wonderfully accepting mother.

Andry, A. and S. Schepp. *How Babies Are Made.* Information provided in a developmentally appropriate way. Suitable for shoring up parents' knowledge or reading with the child.

Bang, M. *Ten Nine Eight.* A father puts his daughter to bed. Doubles as a counting book.

Behrens, J. *I Can Be a Truck Driver.* Both men and women can drive trucks.

Brown, M. *The Runaway Bunny.* Depicts the enduring tie between mother and child.

Caines, J. *Just Us Women.* Female bonding on a car trip down South.

Davol, M. *Black, White, Just Right!* Story of an interracial family.

Dorros, A. *Abuela.* A flight of fancy (literally) with a special grandmother. Gorgeous illustrations.

Greenberg, M. *My Father's Luncheonette.* A proud daughter narrates a behind-the-scenes look at her father's restaurant.

Hoban, R. *A Baby Sister for Frances.* Frances feels ignored after her baby sister is born.

Lasker, J. *Mothers Can Do Anything.* Women depicted in a variety of jobs and roles.

Mayer, M. *Just Grandma and Me.* A child and his grandmother have special adventures together.

Mayer, M. *The New Baby.* Positive interactions between an older child and his new sibling.

Rogers, F. *The New Baby.* Clear photographs and a simple text show what babies are like.

Sharratt, N. *My Mom and Dad Make Me Laugh.* A child holds his own in a very opinionated family.

Stinson, K. *Mom and Dad Don't Live Together Anymore.* A child's story of divorce.

Wandro, M. *My Daddy Is a Nurse.* Story explores an unusual job for a man.

Williams, V. *A Chair for My Mother.* A warm family story that highlights prosocial behavior.

Wood, A. *Elbert's Bad Word.* Because bad things do happen to good people, Elbert is taught a phrase to help him cope.

Zolotow, C. *William's Doll.* Controversy about a boy who wants a doll.

Fears

Mayer, M. *There's a Nightmare in My Closet.* A boy discovers that his nightmare isn't so scary after all.

Medical Issues

Berenstain, S., and J. Berenstain. *The Berenstain Bears Go to the Doctor.* Highlights of a bear medical visit. Cartoon-like illustrations.

Rogers, F. *Going to the Dentist. Going to the Doctor.* Photographs and simple texts provide a detailed and realistic view of an office visit.

Moving

Ballard, R. *Good-Bye, House.* A child says good-bye to each room before she moves away.

Carlstrom, C. *I'm Not Moving, Mama!* A little mouse will miss all the familiar things from his old house.

Rogers, F. *Moving.* A comprehensive look at the issue helps a child know what to expect.

People with Differences

Asletine, L., and E. Mueller. *I'm Deaf and It's Okay.* A hearing-impaired teenager helps a younger child.

Brown, T. *Someone Special, Just Like You.* Wonderful photographs of active children with disabilities.

Caseley, J. *Harry and Willy and Carrothead.* The hero of this story is a boy who was born without a hand.

Cowen-Fletcher, J. *Mama Zooms.* Mother's being in a wheelchair is no barrier to a loving and fun-filled relationship.

Powers, M. *Our Teacher's in a Wheelchair.* A well-balanced story in photographs that does not shrink from the drawbacks of being wheelchair bound as it depicts the competencies of a superb preschool teacher.

Rabe, B. *Where's Chimpy?* A warm and tender look at a father helping his daughter, a Down syndrome child, get ready for bed. Children notice more similarities than differences.

Wild, M. *All the Better to See You.* A young girl needs glasses.

Preschool

Cohen, M. *Will I Have a Friend?* The classic story about preschool jitters.

General

Baker, K. *Hide and Snake.* Find the snake in each of the beautiful illustrations.

Barlowe, D., and S. Barlowe. *Dinosaurs.* A fact-filled dinosaur pop-up book.

Barrett, J. *Cloudy with a Chance of Meatballs.* A book that stimulates both the imagination and the funny bone.

Base, G. *Animalia.* A stunning alphabet book.

Brett, J. *The Mitten.* A group of animals huddle together in a mitten. Breathtaking illustrations.

Brown, K. *Nellie's Knot.* Nellie, the elephant, can't remember why she tied a knot in her trunk.

Brown, M. *The Dream Book.* People's and animals' dreams revealed in a rhyming text.

Carle, E. *The Very Quiet Cricket.* Rhythmic text, glorious illustrations, and a surprise ending.

Carlson, N. *I Like Me.* A book that promotes positive self-esteem.

Carlstrom, N. *Jesse Bear, What Will You Wear?* A little bear's day in a rhyming text.

Carter, D. *How Many Bugs in a Box?* An ingenious pop-up book that doubles as a counting book.

Day, A. *Good Dog, Carl.* Baby and dog home alone. Wordless book, wonderful illustrations.

Degen, B. *Jamberry*. Joyful, rhyming text with just the right touch of silliness.

Ehlert, L. *Red Leaf, Yellow Leaf*. Life of a maple tree. Visually stunning.

Feelings, M. *Jambo Means Hello*. An easy Swahili vocabulary book.

Freeman, D. *Corduroy*. A bear without a button finds a friend.

Greenfield, E. *Honey, I Love*. Volume of loving poetry.

Hoban, R. *Bedtime for Frances*. Frances's parents provide reassurance concerning her nighttime fears.

Itadithi, M. *Hot Hippo*. Story of how the hippo came to live in the water.

Keats, E. *A Letter for Amy*. Peter wants to invite Amy to his birthday party.

Lionni, L. *Swimmy*. Fish organize to outwit a bully.

Loh, M. *Tucking Mommy In*. A sweet role-reversal story.

Martin, B. *Brown Bear, Brown Bear, What Do You See?* Reinforces a knowledge of colors with a captivating rhythmic text.

McCloskey, R. *Make Way for Ducklings*. A classic about a family of ducks in Boston.

McDermott, G. *Anansi the Spider*. African folk tales with beautiful illustrations.

Numeroff, L. *If You Give a Mouse a Cookie*. Giving a mouse a cookie sets off a clever cascade of events.

Piekowski, J. *Oh My a Fly!* Rendition of the classic folk song with ingenious pop-ups and a repeating text that children love.

Pfister, M. *The Rainbow Fish*. A story about sharing, beautifully rendered.

Rey, H. A. *Curious George*. Children want to follow all the adventures of the monkey who is always getting into trouble.

Dr. Seuss, *Horton Hatches the Egg*. A story of loyalty and persistence rewarded.

Siebert, D. *Truck Song*. A truck's trip in rhyme.

Slobodkina, E. *Caps for Sale*. A classic that lends itself to dramatization.

Tafuri, N. *Junglewalk*. A gorgeous wordless book particularly for animal lovers.

Walsh, E. *Hop Jump*. A must for visually oriented frog lovers.

INDEX

DISCARDED